SHEENA TANNA-SHAH

The Power of Being Perfectly
Imperfect

Copyright © 2024 Sheena Tanna-Shah

The moral right of the author has been asserted.

Apart from any fair dealing for the purposes of research or private study, or criticism or review, as permitted under the Copyright, Designs and Patents Act 1988, this publication may only be reproduced, stored or transmitted, in any form or by any means, with the prior permission in writing of the publishers, or in the case of reprographic reproduction in accordance with the terms of licences issued by the Copyright Licensing Agency. Enquiries concerning reproduction outside those terms should be sent to the publishers.

Troubador Publishing Ltd
Unit E2 Airfield Business Park,
Harrison Road, Market Harborough,
Leicestershire. LE16 7UL
Tel: 0116 2792299
Email: books@troubador.co.uk
Web: www.troubador.co.uk

ISBN 978 1805142 942

British Library Cataloguing in Publication Data.
A catalogue record for this book is available from the British Library.

Printed and bound by CPI Group (UK) Ltd, Croydon, CR0 4YY
Typeset in 10pt Avenir by Troubador Publishing Ltd, Leicester, UK

Dedication

This book is dedicated to my parents for all their teachings and love, and to my husband Piyus and daughters Sienna and Isla for their unconditional and endless love, energy and support.

Thank you to all the readers for your support and for allowing me to share my words with you all. This quotation resonated with me during the journey:

Writing allows for inner meditation and mass communication
(S.B. Keshava Swami)

Contents

Foreword	vii
Introduction	ix
Happiness is an inside job	1
The brain and the subconscious mind	7
Raise your vibration	25
Your inner child	31
Trauma	47
Reframing thoughts	53
Anxiety, stress and well-being	58
Flow, not force	66
Face it until you make it	76
Forgiveness	87
Expecting the world to be our version of perfect	100
Imposter syndrome	109
Why me?	116

Being enough	125
Why is it so hard to be happy?	134
Embrace your perfectly imperfect self	142
All aboard the train of life	146
Being open and honest with yourself and others	155
Fear of what others think	162
Relationships with a partner	169
Can you be happy for someone else without feeling sad for yourself?	178
Life will test you until you learn the lesson it's trying to teach you: life triggers	182
Doing nothing is doing something	190
Manifestation	198
Inner thoughts and inner peace	210
Expect the unexpected	216
Positive affirmations	221
Gratitude	232
Meditation	243
Mindfulness	258
The power of sleep	267
The power of nutrition	277
The power of exercise	283
The power of visualisation	287
Hormone hacks	292
The power of journaling	296
Embrace your perfectly imperfect self: revisited	301
Now what?	305

Foreword

We need to hear human stories – of struggle, search, discovery, determination, awakening and achievement. In this book, Sheena gives us a glimpse into the invisible world that most people neglect. As one famous adage reminds us: 'Don't just create a life that looks good on the outside; create one that feels good on the inside.' Sheena's empowering insights give us an opportunity to put that into practice, and we should thank her for putting her lessons from life into an accessible format for one and all.

S.B. Keshava Swami
Speaker, Author & Spiritual Advisor

Introduction

Are you someone who is always searching for happiness?

Happiness can be defined in many ways, but it is usually understood to involve experiencing positive emotions and feeling satisfaction about one's life.

Scientists have found that the three things that make people most happy are pleasure (doing things you enjoy), engagement (feeling interested in your activities and connected to others) and meaning (feeling as if what you do matters), and these can be related to the phrase 'the pursuit of happiness' – a phrase coined by Thomas Jefferson – which exhorts us to pursue a meaningful life that gives us a sense of satisfaction and to do something that is worth living for.

Are you somebody who is searching for that feeling of happiness? Are you somebody who loves motivational quotations, who listens to inspiring podcasts or reads uplifting books to help you on your journey to happiness?

Are you someone who really tries to be positive and upbeat but feels that something still holds you back? Do certain people still emotionally trigger you? Does life have a habit of throwing things in your way? Does the past that no longer serves you keep resurfacing? Do the self-doubts still find a way of creeping in? When things are going well, do you begin to wonder what's going to go wrong? And when things go wrong, do you wonder when will life give you a break?

Do you struggle to feel at peace and at ease with life, often wondering why it seems so hard to feel happy… and stay happy?

If you have answered yes to any of these questions or you resonate with some of them, then I have good news because I UNDERSTAND YOU. I really do, because this was also me once upon a time.

I wanted nothing more than to be happy. Not a huge ask, right? Instead, my anxiety and depression kept following me around: sometimes they would take a vacation but then return refreshed and recharged, ready to overwhelm and consume me again. For you, it may not necessarily be anxiety, but there will be *something* that is preventing you from being truly happy.

My anxiety was present from a young age, although back then (when there was literally zero awareness around well-being), I had never even heard of the word and didn't realise I was struggling. However, as I looked back over the years, I realised my confidence was always at a low ebb; I feared judgement and never thought I was good enough. I would dread things like school assemblies or going on a bus – in fact, any social situations; I was afraid of people looking at me and judging me ... all because I had been constantly told that I needed to smile more, that I always looked miserable, that I wasn't chatty or bubbly enough, that I talked too fast and walked like a robot. The comments were hurtful and made me self-conscious, and I didn't want to walk into social situations and risk hearing those words and being judged again. There was certainly no such thing as self-love back then.

Over my childhood and teenage years and as my confidence took a dive, without realising it, I constantly searched for praise and validation from others. The only guaranteed praise I would get would be from teachers, as I was super studious and relished the positive feedback – 'excellent work' or '10/10'. However, as the years went by, I constantly needed validation from others to fill this huge void. The issue was that I always felt no one liked me because there was nothing to like, and then the cycle of anxiety would kick in. It felt like everyone else was better than me in some way or another. As I reached adulthood, I began to fill the void within me with days out, comfort eating, buying treats, etc., but all this did was give me temporary relief from my unhappiness.

I was always searching for something or someone to make me feel good, to make me feel valid and enough; instead, as I looked around at all these confident, content, successful people who appeared to have their lives together, it made me not only wish I was them, but also feel I was not good enough in any role. Over the years in my various roles, I didn't feel a good enough wife, daughter, sister, mum, optometrist or friend. I didn't feel like I was funny enough, smart enough, pretty enough, slim enough, social enough, confident enough or anything enough. These thought patterns would lead to my mood being up and down constantly; my emotions would range from sad and down to angry and frustrated, with minor moments of respite where I wasn't feeling anything. Any happiness I felt was equal to the external factor causing it: a night away equalled a night of surface-level happiness; a meal out led to a two-hour window of feeling okay before I went downhill again on the roller coaster.

Breaking up with my very first boyfriend at eighteen almost tipped me over the edge. He had been the unhealthy glue that was holding me together; I felt that I must be okay if someone wanted to be with me … until after two years, he didn't. Prior to breaking up, we had decided to do the same university degree in optometry and chose the same university; that first year at university was one of my lowest periods. A time of making new friends and having new experiences was something I couldn't cope with; I was feeling depressed, my social anxiety was spiralling, and I was failing in my studies (you could say the latter was definitely a new experience for me). I really saw no way out, no future and no hope.

I nearly quit my degree and nearly quit every other part of me too. Hitting what felt like rock bottom and waking up in a hospital bed alone and scared led to me seeking professional help for the very first time. Coming from an Indian culture (at a time when we didn't talk about feelings), I could never truly and fully explain my emotions and thoughts, and I felt like a failure in my family's eyes. Why couldn't I be 'normal' like the rest of my family, who didn't cause any dramas or seem to have any issues like me? Why was I the way I was? It was a question that would haunt me daily. I never shared my thoughts with any of my family and friends, and on the outside, they saw me as being that same quiet, moody unsociable person.

I met my husband, who was my absolute rock: his endless patience, encouragement and love supported my healing journey. I really struggled in the early years of our marriage; I was lonely in a new town, and this continued to trigger my deep insecurities. Making new friends was emotionally draining, as I would constantly question myself: 'Do they like me?' 'Why aren't they messaging me?' 'Have I done something wrong?' 'What if I'm not fun enough when we meet up?' and so on. I continued to try various therapies to support my journey.

When I had my children, my anxiety began to spiral. I knew I had to do something; I couldn't be this crying wreck of a mum on a daily basis. I was afraid to go out to any children's classes, I dreaded the school run, I constantly compared myself with other mums – all because of my fear of judgement and my anxiety. My mood was impacting the whole family, and it had to change; that's when I began doing the inner work. I began to face myself and my past, and with a lot of daily mindset work and support, my life began to undergo a transformation. I realised my happiness was my responsibility and mine alone. I also realised I had this belief that 'something' would heal me: when I got my degree, maybe then I would be happy, or I would be happy when I got married, or when I bought my first home, or when I went on the dream trip, etc. And at times, I was happy. But it didn't last.

Everything I learnt, everything I did, everything I discovered and studied to deepen my knowledge and mindset I have put into this book to help you.

You see, I thought I was destined to be the way I was for life; I didn't think that I could change or that I even knew where to begin. I thought that how I was, the thoughts I had and the way I lived would remain like that. I had been this way for too long; change was surely not possible for someone like me. Well, I can tell you I changed in ways I didn't ever envision, I accomplished things I never thought possible, and I embraced myself in a way I never thought I would. I found a happiness within me that isn't temporary but instead continues to grow and strengthen, and if all this happened for someone like me, then it can absolutely happen for YOU. I wasn't one of those 'lucky' ones; I didn't have a sudden epiphany or overnight transformation: no, it took time. I had to get to know myself, face my past and work on my issues every day. This book isn't a magical instant cure, but it absolutely can provide consistent results if you are willing to commit, read, absorb what is here and put things into daily practice. The power of inner happiness really is available to ALL of you.

You may say, 'But Sheena, you don't know me or my

story.' Yes, this is true, but in response, all I will say is that even though your story may be different, all I need to know is the answer to this question: 'Do you want to feel good again in this present moment and feel happy, without that happiness depending on anything or anyone?' If the answer is yes, then you have everything to gain by continuing with the chapters ahead. Your past doesn't have to define your present, but your present can change your future.

Happiness is an inside job

Everything starts with you ... Okay, I understand that when you see those four words it can feel like a huge responsibility, but the truth is that your happiness is ultimately your responsibility (okay, I know that sounds a little daunting, but see it as empowering instead). We often confuse ourselves by believing our happiness is a result of other people's actions or of certain situations working in our favour. Therefore, if other people have hurt you or are continuing to do so, then, surely, they are responsible for you not being happy. Is it a family member, a friend or a partner who's not meeting your expectations or giving you as much as you believe they should and therefore making you unhappy? Maybe you also believe that only by achieving or obtaining certain things you will be happy: when you get that job promotion, perhaps, or when you move into a bigger space, or when you meet your dream partner. Maybe happiness arrives when you think of sandy beaches, blue skies, financial freedom and success.

Let's be clear: that extra space, job promotion, vacation or person is not responsible for your happiness. Yes, the space may offer you extra comfort; the promotion promises to give you a better role and maybe some extra financial security; the vacation represents a break from your normal routine and surroundings; that new person is nice to have around. But have you noticed that when you finally achieve things that you thought would make you happy, the goalposts only get wider and the happiness you feel doesn't last? And very soon, you are on the search again. 'What about those palm-fringed beaches?' you ask. Well, are all those people living on beautiful, sunny islands happy all the time? 'Yes, but Sheena, I wouldn't be working. I would be sipping cocktails every day and relaxing!' Okay. And do you think doing that every day will make you happy? That the novelty won't wear off, that you wouldn't get bored or be keen to do something different at some point, that the bliss and happiness you initially felt wouldn't begin to fade?

The happiness part ... that is on you, and it comes from within you. You can travel the world and accumulate amazing things that give you fragments of happiness that may last days or even months, but it is still temporary because *HAPPINESS IS AN INSIDE JOB*. The pursuit of happiness isn't out there; it is within, and everything external is simply a bonus.

So, let's get excited about that fact because it's actually an exhilarating and liberating feeling knowing that no one and nothing can mess with your happiness.

That's right. Your past, those people, your career, your weight, your age, your wealth, your role – absolutely none of those things define your true happiness. Your happiness stems from your heart and mindset.

You have to put the work in; you have to have the commitment and determination just as with any goal you want to achieve. But if you want happiness, it's yours to feel and have.

Well-being exercise

One of the key steps in rediscovering your happiness is exploring what makes you unhappy. I say 'rediscovering' because as a baby, you were born happy and you were born feeling enough; for example, when you were learning to walk, you fell down multiple times, but you didn't feel judged; you simply tried again. When you didn't want to eat food, you happily threw it on the floor or gestured 'no' by refusing to eat, without worrying that you would be loved any less. In your very early months, you felt content, free and enough just being you; it was the life experiences that you took on board that made you unhappy (more about this later). Acknowledging what makes you feel unhappy and then facing it and processing it will allow you to release it.

Take a moment here to write down some of the things that you feel cause your unhappiness. Some may be obvious things, and some you may actually discover as you go through this book; things that may be stored in your subconscious mind may begin to surface.

Your concerns might relate to your work, your relationship, certain people, finances, health, etc.: however small or large they are, write them all down.

Once you have written these things down, I want you to envisage your beautiful being in the centre of a circle and those things on your list that have happened or are happening outside of the circle. You in the centre are a beautiful force of energy; no one can impact or touch you unless you allow it. This is your space and your energy to preserve; only you have control over it – not anything or anyone else.

You can observe those things from within your circle, and as we work on them, know that you are standing strong in the centre, in control and not being consumed by them. They are out there ready to be faced and responded to, but they are not within you: you have that power.

As you imagine yourself in the centre of this circle, see yourself standing tall and strong, looking straight ahead with clear, focused eyes, wearing bright, beautiful clothes and all the while being filled with a golden light.

See the words describing those areas causing you any unhappiness fading away: the words appear faint and small; you, in comparison, are strong and bold.

You will soon realise that you are the creator of your energy, your day and your life.

I also want you to now get a piece of A3 or A4 paper and some marker pens, and write down on the paper in big, bold, colourful writing the following words:

HAPPINESS IS AVAILABLE TO ME

Now place this paper where you can see it: on a wall in your room, say, or on the fridge or on a desk so that you are always reminded of this message and so that it continues to be absorbed by your mind.

The brain and the subconscious mind

Before we continue, I think it is really important that we understand our physical body, our brain and our subconscious mind because these play a huge role in our well-being. We think about our feelings and emotions, and these all stem from somewhere within our body, so the more we understand ourselves in every way possible, the more effectively we can make the necessary changes to be happier within ourselves.

Sigmund Freud introduced the three-level mind model consisting of the subconscious mind, the conscious mind and the unconscious mind.

The conscious mind is where we experience our thoughts, emotions and actions on a present level. We are very much aware of what is happening and what we are seeing, hearing and feeling: we might, for example, enjoy the sound of birds singing or the taste of freshly brewed coffee. Our conscious mind is also creative and able to learn from everything we see and experience, whether that's reading a book or watching somebody do something. The conscious mind is responsible for rational and logical thinking, decision-making and planning.

The subconscious mind is responsible for our involuntary actions; it stores information from our past experiences, creating our beliefs and also controlling our instant actions and reactions, which occur automatically and without conscious thought; however, if we are required to think about where our actions come from, we can do so. A straightforward example is learning to drive: we learn the skills we need to drive and are consciously aware of the right things to do during our training. However, once we become skilled enough, we do things on autopilot as the subconscious mind takes over; we automatically know which manoeuvres to make and when to look in the mirror without really having to think about it. Have you ever reached a destination and wondered how you got there? The subconscious mind is also responsible for breathing, digestion, memory, emotions and beliefs.

The unconscious mind is where our past experiences lie. They aren't easily accessible to us; for example, trying to recall our first words is challenging.

I want to talk more about our subconscious mind because this really is where the magic can happen. If we understand how the subconscious works and how it impacts our everyday routines, we can then make life-enhancing changes.

The subconscious mind is like a huge databank, storing information from the minute you were born to where you are now: all your memories, everything you heard, everything you saw and all that you felt during your past experiences. How your parents were with you and made you feel; how you felt during your school years; your emotions when you had to take part in a school performance that you hated; your feelings when you passed all your exams; the times when you were compared with your siblings, when your teacher made you feel small, when you first started dating or when you got a job promotion; etc. Absolutely everything – the good, the bad and everything in between – is stored in your subconscious mind. Nothing is deleted, and therefore over time, your belief system starts to shape itself, basing its development on all this stored information.

Our subconscious mind develops primarily from birth until we are about seven years old. We accept all the information around us without questioning it because at this age, we simply believe the words we hear and the experiences we undergo, as we have no reason to question any of it. From our experiences at home with our carers or parents or at school with friends and teachers, we may acquire beliefs such as 'I am not good enough', 'My siblings are better than me', 'I was never wanted', 'I have to work hard to be happy', 'I am unattractive', 'I am no good at sports', etc. We adopt these beliefs and then tune our mind in to further experiencing and confirming them: a job setback falsely confirms that we aren't good enough instead of illustrating the reality that we may need to learn new skills so that we can get the job next time; a first-time class at the gym may cause us to believe that we are not good at exercising rather than remind us of the fact that this is our first class and it takes time to improve.

We become triggered by certain situations and people: even when you are an adult, if your parent still does not give you praise, that can be a trigger, evoking the feelings embedded in childhood of still not being good enough. When you do a new exercise and you aren't great at it, your brain supports the belief that you aren't good at sports – something you have been telling yourself since sports days at school. It doesn't automatically distinguish between facts and beliefs – the fact being that this is a new class and it takes time to learn and improve. Your brain simply accepts every suggestion you give it without question, but not only that: it will find further information to support your thoughts and therefore cause you to view situations with that perspective in mind rather than logic or facts. The more you keep telling your brain the same things over and over – things such as 'I am no good at …' or 'I am always failing at …' – the more firmly these beliefs become entrenched in your brain's neural pathways.

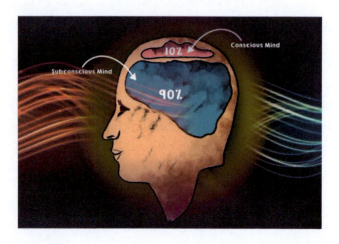

It is therefore very important to start reframing thoughts and changing negative emotions and dialogues to positive ones. I say 'reframing' because all your feelings are valid, but reframing can help change your perspective to serve you better. Usually, we focus on negative emotions, and negative beliefs therefore continue to become stronger and more firmly cemented. For example, when you drive on the same route every day, the road becomes very familiar; it becomes automatic to use that route for your journey, as you are so familiar with it and trust it to get you to where you need to be. The same happens with your thoughts when you persist in the same beliefs – for example, telling yourself that you aren't good at public speaking or that you will never get promoted. These beliefs become automatic and familiar, and they prevent you from trying new ways or giving things a go. Your subconscious doesn't know the truth; it believes every single thing you tell it. If you tell yourself you are unattractive, unlovable, terrible at your job, not confident, not worthy, etc., it will believe you because these beliefs are supported by strong emotions such as disappointment, hurt and sadness. The brain likes being familiar and comfortable, even if the familiarity isn't serving our purpose. It is therefore our job to make the unfamiliar familiar so we can create positive changes from within to live more happily.

The great news is that we can upgrade and transform our subconscious mind; we can rewire our neural pathways and give ourselves beliefs that do serve us better in our life. We can create changes within ourselves; we can start to feel, act and be everything we desire to be; we no longer have to believe that we are chained to our past or that transformation isn't possible or available to us, because it absolutely is. Just as we upgrade our phones, homes, cars and clothes, it's important to upgrade our subconscious mind.

Here are some of the ways you can begin to change your subconscious programming:

1. Be clear with your intention and vision. What is it you want to feel, be and achieve in your future? Focus on this vision without any distracting thoughts or 'what ifs' and 'yes, buts'; be completely free in your thoughts, letting go of any doubts and limiting beliefs. Take a moment to really visualise this, to experience it as if it's already happening. What is it you wish for emotionally and physically in your internal world and your external world? (There's more on visualisation in a later chapter.)

2. Reframe your thoughts in everything you do especially where something is holding you back through fear. Fear of failing, fear of rejection, fear of not being good enough, fear of hurt and embarrassment: fear is one of the biggest things that will hold you back, but you don't have to let it do that any longer. Instead of telling yourself you can't do that public presentation, reframe it, and

say you *can* do it because you have the knowledge, you have prepared yourself and the audience can't wait to hear what you have to say. When you criticise yourself for looking overweight in a certain outfit, tell yourself this: 'I thank my body for looking after me daily, and I am going to make small changes every day to strengthen and nourish it.' Be mindful, and notice your dialogue every day. How often are you feeding yourself negative thoughts such as *I can't do this*? Every time you notice yourself saying this, reframe it. When I am working on a presentation and the doubts come in, I reframe my thoughts and tell myself that I am writing the best information I can from everything I have learnt and continue to learn. I am giving it my all, and that is good enough. It doesn't make me complacent but encourages me to keep going instead of quitting.

3. Set your goals, and work towards them, expecting and embracing setbacks. Open your mind and heart to the notion that setbacks will be part of the course; feel excited and determined by them; trust that you will see it through, that you will find a new way, that there will be a different solution.

4. Be mindful of your external environment, including the people you surround yourself with. Your subconscious mind is constantly absorbing information from your external world and continuing to form beliefs and support older beliefs that are

not beneficial to you. When you get absorbed in comparing your life with the lives of others on social media or become involved in an environment that is toxic, you hinder your transformation. Start by making changes; create an uplifting and peaceful environment that gives you feelings of joy. Listen to podcasts or read inspiring books. Surround yourself with people who are supportive, and reduce the time you spend with people who are not. If certain people cause triggers or hurt, avoid them. Do everything it takes to support your journey.

5. Every time a thought is created, a physical reaction takes place, where focus is placed on positive thoughts; this starts to cause changes in the brain's neural pathways. Working on positive affirmations is a great way of empowering our beliefs and allowing us to focus our thoughts and energy on what we are capable of, inviting abundance into our life. There is a whole chapter on positive affirmations later.

6. Keep reminding yourself that you are no longer your past and that today is a new day to make new progress. Your only mission is to be kinder to yourself and keep working on yourself.

How do you know if you are reprogramming your subconscious mind?

You will be much more aware of yourself, your language, your self-talk, your actions, your responses and how you feel day-to-day.

You will notice you are much kinder and more patient with yourself, you won't take any disappointments personally, and you will recover from any setbacks that come your way a lot more quickly than before. You will have feelings of gratitude and hope about your present and future, and you will no longer feel defined by your past.

Your focus is very much on the present moment, developing a growth mindset where you are open to learning and improving, believing that you can do anything, rather than having a fixed mindset where you believe your skills and goals have limits.

You will begin to feel much more at ease and at peace with your life and everything you are working towards. Your hope and courage in trying new things and effecting the change you want to see will be far stronger than the fear and anxiety that threaten to stop you.

Okay, let's talk a little about our nervous system. Our body has an autonomic nervous system that has two branches: the parasympathetic nervous system and the sympathetic nervous system.

The parasympathetic nervous system is responsible for rest, relaxation, calm, digestion and recharging, whereas the sympathetic nervous system manages our stress response and our awareness of danger by controlling our heart rate, cortisol production, adrenaline secretion, etc.

Ideally, when the parasympathetic nervous system is functioning optimally, we are in a state of calm and our body is able to repair and regenerate itself physically and mentally. However, owing to daily stresses and pressures, many of us are continually activating the sympathetic nervous system, where we are physiologically in fight or flight mode, getting ready to tackle a menacing situation or run away from it. Being in this mode was beneficial thousands of years ago when we faced unpredictable, life-threatening dangers such as wild animals. However, as evolution progressed, our brains didn't catch up as quickly, and so we perceive daily stresses, such as work deadlines, traffic jams, being stuck in a queue or exams, as life-threatening. Therefore, our bodies are constantly in a state of stress and getting ready to tackle these situations in fight or flight mode.

A dysregulated nervous system that is constantly verging on overreacting to these daily stresses can lead to mental health conditions such as anxiety, depression and overwhelming fear, which in turn cause physical health symptoms – headaches, insomnia, irritable bowel syndrome, muscle aches, high blood pressure, etc.

Something that is important to our well-being is the vagus nerve, which is the longest nerve of the autonomic nervous system. The vagus nerve picks up information from various organs such as the heart, lungs, liver and intestines and sends the information to the brain, which in turn analyses and processes it before sending messages back to the organs to instruct them to function in a certain way. It plays a key role in the parasympathetic nervous system in balancing fight or flight responses.

The activity of the vagus nerve – vagal tone – affects the extent to which the sympathetic or parasympathetic nervous system is activated. A strong vagal tone means your body is able to respond better to situations; it is able to regulate your heart rate and blood glucose levels and ultimately keep you in a state of calm. A weak vagal tone means the vagus nerve isn't functioning as well as it could, and this therefore leads to a heightened stress response resulting in anxiety, panic attacks, depression, inflammation and gut issues.

There are many ways we can support our vagus nerve to help us mentally and physically. One of these ways is focusing on our breathwork. Breathing is part of our autonomic nervous system; it is done automatically without us thinking about it. However, we can also control our breathwork and use it to our advantage: by taking deep inhalations into our abdomen and making even longer exhalations, we can stimulate the vagus nerve and the parasympathetic nervous system.

As a little exercise to see how you are breathing right now, I invite you to put one hand on your stomach and one hand on your chest. Close your eyes and breathe normally. Take a moment to check which of your hands is moving more: the hand on your chest or the hand on your stomach.

If the hand on your chest is moving more, this is called shallow breathing, or chest breathing; if the hand on your stomach is moving more, this is called deep breathing, or abdominal breathing. So, what does that mean?

If you happen to be doing chest breathing (which is quite common), you are in a cycle of stress, anticipating the next moment in your day, getting ready either to fight or to flee from the situation. Short, shallow breaths keep our adrenaline running, our pupils dilated and our heart beating faster so we can react quickly.

Being in this cycle of stress isn't healthy for the mind or the body: the over-release of cortisol and adrenaline can impact many things, including our immune system. Also, being highly stressed doesn't make us feel good; we constantly feel as if we are putting fires out instead of enjoying the day peacefully.

Deep abdominal breathing means your brain is being instructed to relax and stay calm by the activation of the parasympathetic nervous system, which allows you to respond, rather than react, and think about situations with clarity and presence, rather than be rushed and chaotic.

Gargling with water, singing and chanting can help stimulate the vagus nerve by vibrating the muscle fibres at the back of the mouth where part of the vagus nerve is located.

Reprogramming the subconscious mind where past trauma may be held and practising meditation are further ways to stimulate the vagus nerve.

In summary, we need to do everything we consciously can to keep our body in a state of calm to support our mental and physical well-being. From the moment we wake up to the moment we go to sleep again, we are faced with information that can lead to stress if we let it. It's our job to control our responses to the day in the best way we can and not let the day control us. The body is powerful in so many incredible ways, and by understanding our home, we can use it to support us in even better ways.

Ego

Ego is the Latin word for 'I'. The concept of the ego has attracted great interest as a result of the work of Sigmund Freud.

In psychoanalytical theory, the ego is defined as the conscious part of us that identifies as 'self' or 'I'. The ego is said to coexist with the 'id' (the part of our make-up responsible for satisfying primitive and basic urges usually involving survival; it doesn't consider logic or rationality) and the 'superego', which acts as the ethical and moral part of the personality and is dependent upon external influences and upbringing.

The ego, according to Freud, acts as a mediator between the inner and outer worlds as well as between the id and the superego. However, without going into too much depth about Freud's work, we can assume the ego is in play when a person's responses involve the terms 'I', 'mine' or 'me' in a situation. Anything that starts with 'I' is your ego: I don't like this, I want to do that, I am going there. We all have an ego, and it is involved in our self-esteem and how we perceive ourselves.

The ego part of ourselves can impact our happiness in many ways; it is important to acknowledge this. When something goes wrong in your life, you may think: *Why did this happen to me?* or *Why did I deserve this?* or *I didn't do anything wrong*, instead of looking at the facts and the reality of the situation.

The ego can start to impact the way you respond to a situation and move forward. Instead of seeing the world as 'I', it's important to start seeing it as an observer. If something goes wrong, instead of thinking *What could I have done?* change your thoughts to *What could have been done?* or *What can be done?* This reduces the thought that everything is in your control or that you are to are to blame and gives you greater clarity on what to do next. We are quick to inflict self-blame, thinking we could have or should have done better or that we should have more control, when the reality is that things are unpredictable and not always in our control. Our ego also makes us believe that only our opinion is right, that we know best, and this leads to the breakdown of relationships. It is important again to be an observer and agree to disagree, to be open to other opinions or to admit we were wrong. Remember that your ego is your identity, whether it's making you feel good or bad; it's that voice in your head that's constantly thinking out loud and forming opinions.

Our ego also wants those that have hurt us to feel the same way as us; for example, if a partner cheats on us, we may want their new relationship to break down, or if someone is unkind to us, we may want them to experience the same feeling back. It can work the other way round too: when we do something nice for someone, do we secretly hope they will do something nice back for us? Our ego creates endless thoughts, and we attach emotions to these thoughts, which then creates a negative living reality – I didn't receive a reply from my friend, I must not be likeable, I am not good enough, I am feeling hurt, I am going to stop making an effort with other people to prevent further hurt – instead of allowing us to frame a positive response: the friend didn't send a reply, but whatever the reason is, that's okay; I can still continue with my day. It sounds simple, but practising this way of thought is vital in not letting our ego take over our lives. Try to become consistently aware of your self-talk.

The ego also labels us as better or worse than others. If you are being healthy and see someone eating junk, you may think *I am better than them*; if you remember your mum's birthday, but your sibling doesn't, you may think you are superior to your brother or sister. If someone gets a promotion before you do, you may think you are not as good as them. We believe we are in one state or the other when in reality we are in neither, and it's so important to remember that. Keep things as neutral, balanced and judgement-free as possible.

Humans also require understanding and reasoning in order to be able to process events and move on; we find it hard to simply accept and let go. When we don't get the answers we want, our anger can start to surface, and this combined with our ego can cause grudges. If this happens, we often start viewing the world in a flippant manner, feeling a sense of anger and frustration with everything and everyone.

You know your ego is taking over when:

- You compare yourself with others;
- You don't like others succeeding;
- You gossip about others;
- You think you are superior to others;
- You subtly show off;
- You make a point of telling people the great work you do, such as charity work;
- You make a point to illustrate your action, saying, for instance: 'I forgave ... I am the bigger person,' instead of just getting on with the action.

These behaviours can impact your happiness, your focus, and your inner healing and progress in the long run.

The reason our ego can take over is that we feel insecure, jealous and envious because underneath we have low self-esteem and low self-worth. Our ego needs to fill the void that's making us question our worth, and so we do or say things in the hope of filling it, whether that's by waiting for likes and validation on a social media post or by making a nice gesture in the hope of receiving something in return. When envy creeps in, we may start to try and outdo other people, make them feel small, deliberately cause hurt to them and do things out of spite to make ourselves feel better, often making a point of showing our status or proving our worth. These are things that don't sound great written on a page, but we may all be guilty of doing them from time to time. However, now is the moment to be honest, to reflect and to question why we are doing that.

When you master your sense of security, and when your self-worth and self-esteem remain at a good, consistent level, then you will begin to master your ego. You will then realise that when you do and say things, they come from a genuine and truthful place, not from a place of ulterior motives.

It's so important to continually train your ego in being non-judgemental; be open to learning and considering different points of view, and accept that you don't know everything and cannot control everything, and that no one owes you anything in life. Let go of control and the need to micromanage it all. Let go of needing external validation, and don't become absorbed in success, power and money. View it all as an observer, and continue doing the good work, being humble and acting from a place of authenticity. Focus on your genuine purpose and not on ego-led issues such as the number of your followers, your superiority, your status, etc.

Question yourself daily. Are you doing this because it looks good to other people or for yourself? Do better than you did yesterday for yourself. No one's words or actions can make you feel bad or question your worth unless you let them; remember that their words are a reflection on them, not you; your focus is working on being your authentic wonderful self.

Raise your vibration

You may hear the phrase 'raise your vibration' a lot these days, but what does that even mean? Understanding our internal vibrations and their effect on us and on the external world can facilitate our journey to inner happiness.

Everything in and around us possesses a form of energy, whether that's a table, a pillow, a plant, a food or a person. Everything is made up of molecules all vibrating at different frequencies. Objects such as a pillow or a table will vibrate at a low energy, whereas a loved and cared-for plant will vibrate at a higher frequency.

A human being is composed of cells made from particles that are in constant motion, all vibrating with energy. Your heartbeats and the breaths that you take are forms of vibration that you can feel and measure, but there are many more tiny vibrations of various frequencies (the speed at which something vibrates is the frequency) occurring within the body that we cannot physically feel. Our behaviour, thoughts and feelings can affect our vibrations.

Our internal vibration will vary depending on our thoughts and actions. We will have low energy when we feel emotions of jealousy, envy, greed, betrayal, anger, hurt, pain, grief, fear, anxiety, etc., and we will have high vibrational energy when our thoughts are purer and have positive characteristics, such as gratitude, joy, contentment, peace, motivation and positivity.

The more we become in tune with our energy, the more we can adjust ourselves to improve it. You will be more conscious when your own energy is low or when you are among people who are vibrating with low energy; it is something you will sense and feel.

Albert Einstein stated that 'everything in life is vibration'.

Have you ever gone to a social event or gathering and, after having spoken to certain people, come away thinking that a certain person gave you good vibes, good energy or a good feeling, or that another person gave out negative vibes and a bad feeling? This is to do with the energy they are radiating and exchanging.

Working on raising our vibration is vital in improving our mental and physical state. When we do, we have more clarity, energy and love, and we feel a stronger sense of happiness from within. This alignment supports our visions and dreams, and manifestation becomes easier too.

When our vibrations are high, we feel light and uplifted, and the journey flows more easily; when our energy is low, we feel heavy, as if we are carrying a weight on our shoulders.

As we become more in tune with ourselves, we will consciously become much more aware of when we are vibrating at either a high or a low level. Have you ever had a day when everything is flowing, the traffic lights all turn green, the sun is out, people are being extra nice, you happen to find some extra money in your bag, someone buys you a coffee? That's because you were largely in a good state of mind to start with. The energy was high, your perception was positively placed, and what you were putting out into the world you were receiving back.

When your vibrations are high, your perceptions of people and of the world begin to change. A situation which may have caused you hurt and pain will no longer impact you as much; you will enjoy being in that state of high frequency and flow, and you therefore will protect your energy. You will walk away from people and situations that are not serving your best interests much more quickly, and you will begin to attract those that are in tune with you much more easily.

All those not-cool and secret thoughts we all have – things like gossiping about others, wishing ill on people or wanting to see someone fail – will reduce massively, and when they do cross our mind, it will prick at our conscience harder than ever before. Your own consciousness vibrating higher will elevate your thoughts.

Ways to raise your vibration

- Always start with gratitude

When you are not in a good place, it's usually because of something that hasn't worked out or because someone has impacted you. The opposite of this is remembering what you already have. Being grateful for your body, home, air, food, pets, family, etc. can allow you to feel warm and loved again. Starting from a place of gratitude reduces the hurt and want and replaces it with appreciation.

- Meditation and mindfulness

Letting go of the past and future and focusing on the present reduces fear and anxiety and replaces them with clarity and focus. Grounding yourself and having this mental space can then allow you to make better positive decisions.

- Generosity

The opposite of exhibiting want, need and greed is being giving and generous. So, focus on giving a little time, maybe in checking in with your nearest and dearest. Give your energy and skills to supporting others, helping a charity or a colleague at work. You can spend some of your earnings in treating someone to a coffee or sending a thank-you gift.

- Forgiveness

We hold on to so much in the heart and mind when we blame others, which leads to feelings of hurt, anger and pain. When we learn to forgive, we are clearing these negative energies.

- Nourishment

All food has high and low energy. Food that has been lovingly looked after, grown, nurtured and watered, and organic food certainly, will have vibrational energy. Food such as meat that's processed will have suffered trauma and pain and will have low vibrational energy. This energy is what we are then consuming, and we feel its after-effects. So, choose what nourishes your body wisely.

- Reframe your thoughts

When in a negative mindset, it is important to reframe our words and actions. Our thoughts affect how we feel, and how we feel impacts our vibration.

- Be around supportive people

Attract your tribe, and be around those who raise you up and make you feel good. When people support, encourage and cheer you on through life's ups and downs, this will give you the boost you require to carry on.

We can all do something to raise our vibration and keep it raised. You will experience a change in your life like no other, a sense of excitement and flow that feels great. You will attract an abundance of amazing things into your life that fill you with joy and happiness. This is like the Wi-Fi you use at home: you may not physically see it, but you know it must be there for the internet to work. You may not see the energy vibrating within you, but you will absolutely feel it and see the results of it when it's at a high frequency.

As you look at the various chapters in this book and start to work on yourself you will begin to naturally raise your vibration. There will be dips and low days – healing is never linear – but continue to put the effort in, and your work on your vibrations will progress well.

Your inner child

I want to talk to you about your inner child and how it could be impacting who you are as an adult today.

When you hear the term 'inner child', it's easy to think that's an invitation to reminisce about your childhood, from playing on the swings and enjoying the gadgets and clothes that were on trend to listening to music from the era with your friends. However, when we talk about the inner child, the subject is in fact a lot deeper than that, and once understood, it could explain many of the behaviours and characteristics that you exhibit today.

The inner child is stored in our subconscious mind and reflects both the positive and the negative experiences of childhood. Some of these involve suppressed emotions, needs that weren't met and hurt that was experienced, but the inner child also harbours some of the joy and happiness that you felt too. The subconscious mind stores all information from birth to where you are now, and if certain experiences and feelings were encountered more than others, these will be more firmly embedded in the neural pathways of the brain.

If, as a child, you were never given praise by the adults in your life like teachers or parents, and if you used to long to hear words such as 'I am proud of you' or 'you are doing amazingly' but never received them, as an adult you could still be longing for these words, and as a result, you might continue never to feel that you are doing well enough in any role. You may have had a sibling that you were always compared with, or perhaps a grandparent belittled you, or a family member hurt you with their words or actions. You would have held on to those words and feelings because of the strong impact they had, and if something similar was said to you, or you were made to feel a similar way again later in life by someone else, then this belief of not being good enough would be amplified and strengthened.

You would be telling yourself that they must all be right and you must be wrong; your lack of belief in yourself would continue and carry on in every stage of your life because you would not be telling yourself anything different. Your mind believes what it sees and hears, and you then behave accordingly.

Imagine that a parent tells you that you could have done better in your exam or that your sister did better than you: that would make you feel that you were not good enough. Maybe at school you were always reminded to do better and compared with the clever kid; once again, that confirms the belief that you are not good enough. You now carry this belief in your life going forward, and it affects your future.

Perhaps when you go for interviews or for a driving test, you automatically doubt your ability and fear once again the words or feelings of not being good enough. You dread the test, you panic, and you feel nervous, all because you have been, and still are, trapped in that same narrative stemming from a childhood belief that you aren't good enough.

If you had begun to change the narrative to 'I did my absolute best, and I am going to learn and grow for next time' or 'I am doing my best, and that is enough', then you would have felt more positive about the task and the outcome, believing you gave it everything you could. As a child, we don't always know any different, and in accepting the words and opinions of those around us, we trust that the adults in our life 'know best' and what they are saying must be true. As a child, when we look up to the adults in our life, we not only believe what they are saying, we may also not always have the confidence to voice our own opinions and questions. When we reach adulthood, some of these words are deeply embedded within us, and we are conditioned by them.

Someone else's thoughts and opinions are exactly that: theirs and not yours. However, you have created a belief system stemming from childhood, from a time when you felt your voice or opinion didn't matter. A time when you looked to others for validation, love and security. Often, because you craved that love and attention as a child, you went along with what the adults in your life were saying or doing in an attempt to fit in at an age when you depended on others for approval and a sense of belonging. It was normal to feel these needs as a child, but you carried these beliefs into adulthood where they are no longer serving you, where you do have an opinion and a voice that actually matter, where the only approval and validation you need are yours and yours alone. The only people you need in your life are the ones supporting you, not those discouraging you.

Maybe a teacher made you feel that you didn't do a good job in the school assembly, or a parent said that crying is a weakness, or a friend said you were slow in a school race or never included you: you may have then carried these experiences into your adult life, believing that you aren't good at public speaking, that showing emotions is a sign of weakness, that you are no good at sport and that you will never have good friends. These beliefs are from your inner child and not from the person you are right now. You are holding on to beliefs stemming from childhood that no longer serve you.

When you access your inner child, you begin to identify and understand some of the issues you may be experiencing as an adult. Understanding is a powerful thing; when you understand who you are today and where your thoughts, behaviours and actions stem from, you can begin to process events and rewire your neural pathways.

The inner child may connect you to those playful carefree times, but if you experienced emotional or physical trauma, had a difficult relationship with your parents, etc., then it could be that you are holding on to some of this pain in your present life and that it is impacting your thought process, behavioural patterns and relationships with others and yourself.

Maybe your husband has to work late a few nights. You become enraged and start suspecting he is having an affair. These assumptions that surface aren't based on any facts but on feelings stored in your subconscious mind associated with the time when you found out your father had been having an affair that left your mother devastated; now this has made you suspicious of all men.

Maybe you look around at everyone else getting promoted and moving forward in their careers while you have been in the same position for some time. You don't feel you are good enough and so don't attempt to try to progress; you can't bear rejection, because you experienced it as a child when you never used to get picked for school teams. It made you feel embarrassed and hurt, and you don't want to go through that again. You believe you will hear those words again and they will confirm once more that you aren't capable. Instead of challenging yourself and finding out what you can do to grow and develop, you nurse the belief that it will never happen for you. Not being picked for that school team has no correlation with your work right now, yet it's still impacting your present and your future.

Some children at school may have been mean to you about your appearance, made fun of you or said unkind words. Now every time you look in the mirror, you find fault with yourself: your hair's not right, your clothes don't look good, you wish you were taller or shorter, you believe people have been judging you whenever you step out. So now you avoid going out, and if you do, you try not to draw attention to yourself, perhaps, for example, wearing only clothes that are black or neutral in colour, all because of what someone said at school.

The above scenarios are just examples of how present-day situations can be impacted by childhood experiences; you may start looking at the timeline of your own life and notice some correlations between your past and present.

I remember at school, people would often comment that I walked like a robot and talked too fast; that impacted me so much that I would avoid school assemblies any time there were certificates to collect, as the thought of the walk to the front of the hall was too awful to bear. I would imagine everyone staring at me and whispering. I struggled to get on buses because I would hate people watching me walk along the aisle trying to find a seat, and I shunned social events, as I would hate people watching me enter them or move around. I had created this image in my mind that people were constantly judging me, and it made me feel ultra self-conscious – all because of the impact of people's words in my childhood. This would lead to my social anxiety.

I recall the school nurse weighing me and telling me I would become overweight, and I then recall people at various times in my life telling me I looked 'big' or I had put on weight since we had last met. Coming from an Indian culture, the adults present in much of my early life had no filter; they would literally say what they thought, and if they had an opinion on your appearance, they would let you know. This absolutely impacted my body image and how I felt about my appearance for many years.

I had to work on fathoming my behaviours and where they stemmed from, understanding my inner child and letting go of all those people and words from the past. That person was no longer me; the adult in me embraced the way I walked, talked and looked, and if anyone were to judge me, it would be a reflection on them, not me.

Experiencing some form of emotional neglect as a child, no matter how small it is, can really influence our adult life. Parents will have had their own trauma, stresses and healing to work through, and they would have dealt with that in various ways. They would have had their own lives, roles and emotions to navigate and may not always have been aware of the deeper needs of their child, and even if they were, they may not have had the support, resources or knowledge needed to provide emotional support; theirs was a generation where domestic abuse, substance abuse, and mental and physical abuse were not uncommon and were frequently witnessed by children.

Many parents praise their children only when they achieve something in a misguided attempt to encourage them to keep doing better, without realising that they should be showing love and giving praise regardless of results and achievements. As much as parents can provide unconditional love, there may nevertheless be triggers that can at times cause them to become envious of their children (this may come as a surprise, but it is very much the case in some family situations). Seeing their children having and achieving things that they didn't have or achieve can cause relationship issues, particularly when these emotions haven't been healed. Comments from parents such as 'you've got it easy now', 'you have no idea how lucky you are', and 'I didn't have all this when I was your age' can all be signs of an absence of healing and of the parent being triggered.

For some parents – depending on circumstances – talking about feelings, stepping away from a difficult situation, protecting children and reaching out for help may not have been easy to do. This is definitely not an excuse, as parental responsibility should not be taken lightly, but it is, however, a very sad reality. Awareness of the importance of well-being, as well as the associated support and resources, was much more limited a number of years ago than it is today. Generational trauma is something we have to be aware of and break. Their childhood, life and struggles may have caused them their own pain and hurt, which ultimately also impacted you, but that pain has to end with you.

You may have been brought up in a household where there was zero communication from your parents, or where, if you were ever struggling with anything, you couldn't easily approach them. Maybe, if you ever did speak up or show you were struggling, you were made to feel your emotions were invalid, with comments like 'cheer up, it's not that bad', 'get over it', 'it's not that much of a big deal', 'you don't need to be that upset', 'that's no reason to cry', etc. Parents may simply have dismissed your needs and feelings as irrelevant or insignificant.

You may have had parents who gave only conditional love when you behaved in a certain way, achieved something or acted in a way that fitted in pleasingly with their world view.

I certainly know that, coming from an Indian culture, my parents and many in their generation had really struggled in making ends meet; they had moved to a new country after being forced out of their own; English was a second language; they had faced racial abuse; and they were doing everything they could to simply survive. Their hopes and dreams for their children were high; they didn't want them to struggle the way they had; and often, their relentless determination in ensuring their sons and daughters got good grades and a good education put difficult pressures and expectations on the children. Above all, parents were wedded to the belief that good grades equalled good jobs and that good jobs resulted in happiness and successful lives. Praise, if any, was only given for high academic performance; any other thought, feeling or ambition was routinely dismissed. This often led to careers being chosen under pressure: we felt the need to please our parents constantly and the need to meet their requirements of what success meant, and we were often compared with others along the journey. Again, a misguided attempt to motivate us just made us feel not good enough. Often, we try to live our parents' version of what success and happiness mean when really we need to focus on our own version of those things and not be afraid or feel guilty in doing so.

In your adult life, some signs of emotional childhood neglect include having low self-worth and self-esteem, still seeking praise and validation, especially from parents, feeling that only achieving the best is good enough, self-sabotage, difficulty in understanding why you feel so low and comparing yourself with others. You may also long for deep, loving, emotional relationships with friends or partners but find it difficult to feel content in them; you may find it difficult to express your feelings, which leads to a feeling of being overwhelmed, insecurity, loneliness and a roller coaster of emotions.

It's so important to remember that just because your parents have a biological connection to you, it doesn't mean your happiness is dependent on them and on their validation. As a child, you may have needed their validation because you knew no different, but now as an adult, it's important to know that you can be free from that belief and from their praise, opinion, respect and emotional connection (or the lack of these responses); these things no longer need to control your life.

The way they treated you, intentionally or unintentionally, is a reflection on them, not you. You may have had conversations and confronted them in the past if you felt the need to; the chances are they defended themselves or didn't realise what you were driving at. This probably didn't make things any better for you, so now is the time to take the hardest yet most beneficial step and let it go. You don't need to understand them, and you don't need to tell them how much pain they have caused or find ways to remind or show them, because by doing that you are accepting that they still have control over you; now is your chance to stop wasting any more energy and time on them and live for you.

This really is one of the hardest things to do because your parents have been part of your life from the moment you were born, and so such a huge step will take time to process and to take. You will also have a perception of what an 'ideal' parent looks like and how one should be and behave towards their children – beliefs created from what you see in the movies, how you see other parents behaving towards their kids or how you feel a parent–child relationship should be. Questions about, and understanding of, why your parent couldn't be there for you in the way you needed, why they said and acted the way they did, etc. will all take time to move on from… but it's something you can do.

This can still be difficult mentally even if you hardly see your parents, because it is the mental aspect that is holding you back, not the physical distance between you. It's important to stress that it is not about cutting them off or not speaking to them or seeing them ever again, but more about letting go of the control they hold over you subconsciously. Give yourself the permission to let go. They have continued to live their life, and yet part of your life has been on hold. Can you continue feeling and living this way for the next one, five or ten years? You are an adult now, and you can continue to remind yourself that the parental love you needed as a child is something you no longer need now and that every loving and kind action you desired from them you can give to yourself now instead.

Make your own choices, live your own dreams and ambitions, achieve things for you in your own time without waiting for any recognition or acceptance from them. Do what makes you feel good, and let their judgements and opinions fade away. Give yourself the praise and be your own cheerleader. You no longer need to live in the shadow of their expectations. This moment right here is about you, not them.

If your parents are no longer in your life but you realise they still have a hold over you, have a conversation in your mind with them telling them you are officially letting go of their hold over you. Let them know that despite the hurt they may have caused previously, your childhood is no longer going to impact your present life. Let them know you are letting go of any hurt and resentment and opening up that space instead to more love and abundance in your life. This may feel strange to do, but I urge you to take time out and really give this the time it requires because you deserve to be free from a past that no longer serves you. You can imagine them in front of you and have this conversation out loud, or you can even write them a letter. It really is a powerful thing to do.

These conversations can also apply to absolutely anyone who didn't make you feel great in the past: have that person mentally in front of you if you can, and let them know they no longer control your thoughts or actions. Visualise this person as you let them know their words and actions may have once been hurtful but now you are standing up to them; let them know their words are now insignificant and meaningless and no more of your internal space will be occupied by them. Let them know that you once wanted their acceptance, appreciation, validation or love but you now realise that you never needed it and will never need it again. As a child, it was normal for you to want these things; you were dependent on someone to give you love and make you feel valued, but as an adult, you no longer need this from someone else. That person may have once had control over you, but now the only person controlling you is you; no one has to define you ever again, especially any of those people from the past.

Take a look back along your timeline as far as you can remember, and think about any people or events that may have shaped your beliefs and about who you are today. There will be questions and lots of wondering why, but your happiness is not dependent on the answers. Whether you understand them or not, and whether they understand your hurt or not, it's time to let them go. It's time to put yourself first; it's time to start living and breaking free from these invisible chains of the past. We often want those that hurt us to take responsibility and accountability for their actions; in certain cases this is important. However, your freedom to live peacefully and happily should not depend on this.

As you stand tall and strong, ready to live YOUR life, imagine that person now fading and shrinking away;

imagine them disappearing out of your sight and mind forever. If the trauma is too deep to do this, please seek support from a professional who can help you.

This is a reminder that you are not that child any more and that you are not your past experiences; you are a beautiful being who is ready to live a life filled with an abundance of happiness.

Well-being exercise

Write down a list of things you would have absolutely loved to hear when you were a child. Some examples are:

- I am proud of you
- You are enough
- You are amazing
- You are incredible
- You did a fantastic job
- You are special
- I am always here for you no matter what
- I love you
- I appreciate you
- I will always support you

Feel free to add your own. Once you have done so, I want you to find a comfortable space and take a few deep breaths. Give yourself a hug or give a fist pump, and tell yourself all the things you have written on your list. Tell yourself all the things you longed to hear from someone else, and remind yourself that the most powerful and influential person, and the one whose validation matters most, is YOU.

Tell yourself that you are proud of you, that you matter, that you are loved and supported.

If you haven't already this time, say it out loud; yes, initially it may feel strange, but soon, it will feel liberating and empowering.

Wherever you are in life right now, whatever you

have achieved, you have something to be proud of just by BEING YOU. Whenever you are looking for words or validation from others, as nice as it may be when you get those things, remind yourself that you don't need anything from them; you've got you, and slowly, you will realise that's enough.

Every day, become your own cheerleader; give yourself love, encouragement, and awesome cheers to keep you moving forward.

Inner Child

Trauma

When you hear the word 'trauma', it's easy to think of deep, wounding, long-term hurt and pain, such as grief or abuse. However, you can experience macro- and microtraumas, and everyone will have experienced some form of microtrauma.

Microtraumas are small incidents that have caused hurt and pain for a short period or possibly over a longer period. Microtraumas can include somebody ignoring you, somebody making hurtful comments, insults, people putting you down, ghosting, etc. Small forms of hurt on their own can sometimes be ignored, forgotten about and brushed under the carpet; however, if these small emotional traumas continue to happen over time, then this will slowly start to impact the mindset and belief system. This affects work, relationships and health. Imagine tiny cracks forming in a building. You may ignore them, plaster over them or see them as small and insignificant, but when these cracks become larger and start to unite, you know there is a serious problem.

Macrotraumas are unavoidable, impactful life events, such as the death of a person close to you, abuse, injuries, health issues, accidents, being in a war, divorce, job loss, etc. These are large traumas that you have to face, sometimes suddenly; they can cause deep hurt and pain if they aren't processed and managed, and it can take longer to heal from them.

Acknowledging all levels of trauma is the first step in processing it and being able to navigate through it. Everyone will react differently to trauma, depending on their subjective emotions about the situation and their past experiences and belief systems. If you witness someone reacting less animatedly than you to a certain situation, it doesn't mean they are coping better than you; they are just coping in the only way they know how. For some, it takes time to talk about it and face up to an event; others need to start dealing with it straight away. Some may feel they are coping and managing or decide to ignore it or block it out, but over time, they realise they are struggling and require support. Everyone is different, and that's okay; some of the signs that you may require support include:

- Anxiety and fear
- Regret, guilt and self-blame
- Anger and frustration
- Confusion, shock, disbelief and even denial
- Loneliness and insecurity

- Sadness and hurt
- Insomnia
- Poor concentration and motivation
- Headaches
- Fatigue
- IBS
- Muscle pain

What can happen if we keep experiencing the above signs and symptoms, is that the subconscious mind will once again store these emotions and feelings, which can lead to post-traumatic stress disorder as they become embedded in our nervous system. Your body sees trauma as a sign of danger, and it believes that to give you the best chance of survival, it needs to keep you in 'freeze' mode.

I mentioned fight or flight previously; a third element is freeze. As children, if we were subject to certain traumas and we were not able to tap into our fight or flight response, then we would learn to freeze instead, being immobile and feeling numb and heavy; as adults, we are subject to certain triggers that can still cause us to freeze in the same way.

Certain external factors can cause us to freeze when our brain thinks it is the best way to aid survival. For example, certain physical responses to dangers, such as running away from someone or needing to hide, can cause us to stop and freeze; our heart rate slows down, we hold our breath, and we become very still. At other times, activities such as public speaking or going for an interview may provoke the same response. You may hear people say: 'I froze on the spot.' The brain believes that you are entering a threatening situation (the job interview, for instance), and it therefore tries to help you.

In an abusive relationship, if a partner is shouting and yelling at you, you may either shout back (fight response), walk away (flight response), or become still and start to dissociate and detach from the situation (freeze) until it's over.

There are many different ways to support yourself when you have experienced any form of trauma. Talking about how we are feeling can really help. Releasing our internal thoughts and emotions is a step towards understanding them. Talking to other people who may have gone through similar situations is a really good way of knowing that you are not alone, that your feelings are valid and understood and that there are others who can support you. Often, when talking to people outside of the situation, as much as they care, there are times when you may feel that they just don't get it; in a support group this problem is eliminated.

Talking to a professional will also help, as they will guide you through the various techniques to process situations and move forward in a safe space.

Talking about how you feel may not come easy, because you may not know what to say or where to begin, and you may worry if things don't make sense, as they don't even make sense to you. Equally, you may experience fear of being judged. Sometimes, writing things down can help untangle your thoughts, and then it is helpful to reassure yourself that those you speak to want to listen and help and that whatever doesn't make sense will eventually become clear and that you will find a way forward.

Continuing to engage in other hobbies and activities, exercising and eating well are also important, as is feeling loved and supported by friends and family. Be mindful that you are not isolating yourself from the outside world and those closest to you.

We may not feel like moving, getting up (all part of the freeze coping mechanism) or getting out, wanting instead to hibernate, but movement and exercise are key components of recovery. Reducing cortisol and releasing endorphins will slowly start making you feel good again. Whether it's a walk around the block, a stroll in the park or marching up and down the stairs, doing something daily will make a significant difference in the long term.

Practise meditation and mindfulness to reduce future fear, worry and anxiety, and instead feel more grounded and present in the day.

Ensure self-care is a priority – and that should include managing sleep, nutrition and hydration. If you are struggling in any of these areas, know that you are not alone and that there are plenty of people who can help you, whether it's friends and family or support lines. It takes courage to ask for help, but your future self will thank you for it. Get the support until you are able to find ways to support yourself.

Trauma is a vast topic; it is so important to healing, to living your best life and to finding your inner happiness.

Some of the later chapters in this book discuss further aspects of trauma.

If you have suffered with a traumatic experience, it takes resolve to work on it, but trust that you really have the strength you need within you. You will need to dig deep and survive some uncomfortable moments, but give yourself credit, time and patience. Never give up hope on yourself and your future; your trauma doesn't have to define you.

Take a look at some of the above suggestions. What is the easiest or most convenient thing you can do? Start from there. It may mean just starting the day with a nourishing meal, journaling your thoughts or texting a friend. Small steps will lead to long-term progress. You may have blips and triggers along the way. A memory may pop up, or a certain time of year may be harder than others, but that's okay – you can validate that and still continue the work.

Remember who you were before this trauma; remember that that person still exists and that you've got this. You still deserve to live the very best life, you still deserve to be happy, you still deserve to fulfil your hopes and dreams. Your trauma doesn't have to hold you back or be the thing that limits you; it happened to you, but it doesn't need to *be* you.

Reframing thoughts

How often do you judge and criticise yourself and tell yourself you haven't done enough, you could do more or you could do better? We are often pretty hard on ourselves, our abilities and accomplishments, whether that's in our work or family life, our personal goals or even the daily chores. It's time to start being kinder and nicer to ourselves. We would never let anyone speak to our nearest and dearest the way we do to ourselves, right? So why is it okay to talk to ourselves like that? The answer is that it's not okay; we've just become so used to doing it. But it's time to stop judging and start appreciating our worth, and it starts now. Here is an example of how to go about reframing your thoughts.

When you notice you are being critical of yourself, simply STOP. You can even say it out loud to yourself: 'Hey, STOP.'

Take some deep breaths.

Take a moment to understand where your thoughts

have come from. Have you attached further stories and emotions to them?

Let's use this example:

I am running late this morning. I am always running late. I am never organised. My mum was right about me.

The fact is your thought was based on you running late today; the additional story to this thought was that you recalled other times you were late, and you remembered your mum telling you that you were not organised, and now your emotion is one of not being good enough.

Ask yourself whether thinking this thought serves a purpose for you. Does it make you feel good? Or would it be more productive to do something about it?

Reframe the thought *I am always late* to something resembling the following examples:

I was late today; however, tonight, I am going to prepare my lunch for tomorrow, and I will wake up twenty minutes earlier so that I can have plenty of time to get to work. I am making improvements to better my day.

I am going to be better organised by preparing everything I need tonight and setting my alarm twenty minutes earlier than usual so I have ample time to be ready for work. I am excited to make these changes to improve my day.

Here are some further examples of reframed thoughts.

I am awful at interviews. Reframe this to: *I learnt some useful tips from previous interviews and am going to improve my techniques and excel at future ones.*

I am such a bad parent, always shouting at the kids. Reframe this to: *I am a fantastic parent, and I try my best at all times. I will continue to be mindful of my responses every time.*

I am never good at talking in social events. Reframe this to: *I am a fantastic listener and have valuable knowledge to share, which I will do in my own space and time.*

Well-being exercise

Let's write down some negative thoughts you may have had today or some thoughts you commonly have.

Negative thought:

Story and emotion attached to it:

I can reframe this thought to:

Negative thought:

Story and emotion attached to it:

I can reframe this thought to:

Negative thought:

Story and emotion attached to it:

I can reframe this thought to:

Anxiety, stress and well-being

Stress and anxiety can feel similar at times, but they are very different. They both occur as a result of the fight or flight response getting the body to prepare for a perceived or real threat; however, the extent of our response is what we need to consider.

Many people will have experienced anxiety at some point in their life; however, the level and type of anxiety experienced, and the strategies used to manage it, will vary from person to person.

Anxiety is a feeling of fear, uneasiness, nervousness and uncertainty with regard to a particular situation and its possible outcomes. Anxiety is based on worries about future events that may involve other people, the outcomes of which we can't control.

Anxiety is a normal response when the mind and body feel threatened and get ready to go into fight or flight mode. However, anxiety becomes an issue when we are stuck in this mode for a period of time that is longer than necessary. It is also an issue when the feelings of worry are out of proportion to the actual situation or when we have added extra stories and emotions to the situation that don't serve any purpose. For example, a socially anxious person walking along the street may believe that people are staring at them and judging them, waiting for them to trip or do something wrong, when in reality, they will simply be going about their own business. Anxiety can occur when people worry about their future, their plans or their health, usually focusing on things not working out. When the outcome of a situation is uncertain, an anxious person will create a lot of 'what if' scenarios: 'What if this goes wrong?' 'What if that doesn't work?' 'What if I make a mistake?' etc.

Research has shown that anxiety can be caused by genes and environmental influences, and studies continue. The psychiatric epidemiologist Dr Anna Bauer asserts that there is no single 'anxiety gene', but rather many genes that interact to predispose someone to anxiety; through a biochemical process known as DNA methylation, our environment – what we eat, how we sleep, the air we breathe, the stress we face – can alter the expression of our genes.

According to another researcher in this field, Dr Anthony Zannas, we are 'born with our genetic code, but the environment influences the extent to which those genes will get switched on or off'.

The people we surround ourselves with, the life events that we experience and the belief system and mindset we then create as a result of these external influences can contribute to our anxiety. If from a young age we are in an environment where our parents are highly anxious, constantly telling us not to do something or instilling fear in us, this will create anxiety within us. If they constantly warn us not to drive because the roads are busy and dangerous, or not to go into the sea because a current might drown us, or not to walk alone because someone might hurt us, this will create fear and anxiety within us and a consequent reluctance ever to do these things.

You can experience emotional and physical symptoms when going through anxiety, including a sense of dread, overthinking, a racing heart, shortness of breath, headaches, sweating, dizziness, aches and insomnia. And anxiety becomes an issue when we are consumed by it for long periods and it starts to impact our daily life.

Various problems can cause specific anxiety disorders: a difficult childhood, traumatic past events, abuse, financial issues and other life events. Specific anxiety disorders can be diagnosed when we meet a certain criterion; these disorders include the following:

Generalised Anxiety Disorder (GAD): GAD is characterised by excessive and uncontrollable worry or anxiety about a variety of everyday concerns, such as work, health, family or finances. People with GAD often find it difficult to relax and may experience physical symptoms like restlessness, irritability, muscle tension, fatigue and difficulty concentrating.

Panic Disorder: Panic disorder involves recurring panic attacks, which are sudden episodes of intense fear or discomfort that peak within minutes. Panic attacks can be accompanied by physical symptoms such as heart palpitations, shortness of breath, chest pain, dizziness, trembling and a feeling of impending doom. Individuals with panic disorder often worry about experiencing future panic attacks and may develop agoraphobia (fear of being in places or situations where escape might be difficult).

Social Anxiety Disorder (Social Phobia): Social anxiety disorder is characterised by an intense fear of social situations or performance situations due to a fear of being scrutinised, embarrassed or humiliated by others. People with social anxiety often avoid social situations or endure them with great distress. Physical symptoms may include blushing, sweating, trembling, nausea and difficulty speaking.

Specific Phobias: Specific phobias involve an intense, irrational fear and avoidance of a specific object, situation or activity. Common specific phobias include fear of heights, spiders, flying, injections or certain animals. When confronted with the feared object or situation, individuals may experience immediate anxiety or panic attacks.

Obsessive–Compulsive Disorder (OCD): OCD is characterised by recurring, intrusive thoughts (obsessions) and repetitive behaviours or mental acts (compulsions) aimed at reducing anxiety or preventing a feared event. Common obsessions include concerns about cleanliness, symmetry or harm, while common compulsions may involve excessive handwashing, checking or counting.

Post-Traumatic Stress Disorder (PTSD): PTSD can develop after experiencing or witnessing a traumatic event. Symptoms may include intrusive memories or flashbacks of the trauma, avoidance of reminders of the trauma, negative changes in mood and cognition, hyperarousal and emotional reactivity.

Stress occurs when you are reacting to a challenging situation or an external threat; it then reduces or disappears once the stimulus recedes. You are stressed about your workload, you are stressed by the need to manage your time, you are stressed about your finances, you are stressed about an argument you have just had. Anxiety can be a response to any one of these situations, but it remains long after the situation is resolved, whereas stress has a shorter time frame.

Some level of stress can be good in that it can move you forward to complete a goal or project or it can move you to a safer place and space, but when stress consumes and overwhelms you, it needs to be managed.

High stress can make situations difficult to get through, but you are usually still able to find a way to deal with them; anxiety, on the other hand, can leave you feeling as if you can't cope. You may end up having a panic attack or running away from the situation. You will often feel anxious about events that haven't even happened yet. That internal feeling of dread and worry centres on future situations or events that may not even happen. Stress will always occur in real-life situations.

Small stressors that build up daily – the routine

chores getting on top of us, work pressures, situations with family and friends – can lead to chronic stress, for which there will always be a known cause.

It's so important to manage stress and anxiety because when we don't, they not only impact our mental health further but also begin to cause us physical health issues. It really is about prevention before cure. Become aware of your own signs when you realise you are becoming stressed or anxious, and do something about it before they escalate.

How to manage stress and anxiety:

1. Write down the cause or causes of the stressor. What task or event is causing you to feel this way? Then, start looking at ways to support this situation. See if you can break the task down: ask for support, delegate, do small amounts at a time, take more breaks and rests. The housework, for example: it always piles up and feels never-ending; you're struggling to stay on top of it. Can you ask for more support from those living with you, or get an external person to help?

    Can you allocate certain days and times for certain tasks? For example, Thursday, 45 minutes ironing; Wednesday, 30 minutes hoovering and polishing; Saturday, 60 minutes bathroom cleaning and laundry, etc. Writing tasks down, having a plan and knowing things will get done can really help reduce the stress.

Or, if the stress is caused by a work presentation or project, write down the parts of the task that are stressing you and what can you actively do to reduce your stress. Do you require support from someone? Do you need to prioritise and list what needs doing? Do you need to research or rehearse? Reward yourself for small victories; celebrate the steps of progress, not just the end result.
2. Create boundaries. Maintain a balance between managing what you can do and being able to say no to things that may cause further stress.
3. Have a good support network where you can talk to someone about how you are feeling; it always helps to release the thoughts in our mind and hear a different perspective.
4. Do something that makes you laugh: watch a comedy, read some jokes or get together with friends; this can release endorphins, which are known to relieve stress.
5. Use relaxation techniques such as breathwork, meditation, tranquil music and warm baths to really help calm the mind and body.
6. Celebrate every small win, and be proud of yourself all the way.
7. Practise mindfulness and meditation. Anxiety is having a fear of the unknown and is usually related to the future; therefore, practising mindfulness and being in the present moment can really help.
8. Reframe and challenge your self-talk. What's true, and what is a fabrication of your mind?

9. Take small steps out of your comfort zone; this will help you to start proving to yourself that you are stronger than you realise. Enjoy a coffee in a café with no one but yourself for company; visit a new place; start a new hobby, even if it's a home online activity.
10. Maintain a healthy lifestyle with good sleep, nutrition and exercise, and avoid distracting or numbing coping mechanisms such as alcohol, drugs, overeating, oversleeping, binge-watching TV, etc. (More on this later.)

As someone who struggled with anxiety for years, I know that implementing and practising these self-care tips daily can make a huge change in how you perceive and live your life. It will take time, but the more you train your mind into thinking and living in a new, positive way, the easier it becomes. That's not to say that certain triggers will never cause stress or anxiety, but it does mean you are able to recover and respond much more quickly and much more productively. Instead of letting anxiety consume you, you are able to step back and take control of the situation because the coping mechanisms that you have been practising are ready to take over.

Flow, not force

When we have a dream or a vision, we may put some goals and actions in place to start our journey towards achieving it. We envision a path from where we are to where we want to be, and that's great, but we don't often factor in the idea that there may be setbacks along the way. Think about the last time you wanted to achieve something that involved a plan. Was it all plain sailing? There may have been some bumps in the journey, whether they were minor or major, and they may have thrown you or caused disappointment or frustration or a mixture of emotions.

The brain likes security: it gives us comfort, ease and a sense of being okay, away from hurt, pain and stress. However, by not embracing or factoring in that there is a chance of setbacks and challenges occurring during the journey, you are almost guaranteed to set yourself up for stress, emotional overload and disappointment. This is not to cause you fear or worry before you plan something but to simply invite you to embrace the fact that some plans go smoothly, while others may take a different path; either way, it's a question of surrendering to the journey and the outcome.

Whether you are planning a holiday, a trip to the supermarket or a long-term career goal, there is a possibility of the unexpected happening. There may be delays at the airport, queues at every checkout, or long nights and early starts in your working life. You may have a life plan, where you envision having a certain job by a set age, finding a partner, getting on the property ladder, etc., but again, prepare for the timeline and outcomes to vary. Now, you may feel that's not very positive or optimistic; however, what I would say is that positivity and optimism will play their biggest role when you have to deal with a bump or navigate to a different route.

When you hit those minor or major setbacks – the delays, the people who aren't helpful, the unexpected issue – that is when you will need to respond positively and optimistically rather than with frustration or fear. Think about the last time you had a setback. How much stress did it put you under? Did it impact your mood and emotions? Did you spend more time venting and feeling annoyed than doing something productive or finding a solution? Did you spend time blaming the situation or people rather than looking for support or other resources to help you? Were you trying to force things to move quicker rather than letting events flow?

Ironically, as I write this, I am going through a

setback; a big curveball has come my way. The situation initially threw me, and I took one day to feel sad and to reflect on, reset and validate my emotions, reminding myself it was okay to feel everything I was feeling. Then, I had to fully reset because this was happening, and blaming anyone or anything wouldn't resolve it. I didn't know how the situation would turn out, but I had to continue to follow the steps and work on it, to keep going, relying on the best of my knowledge and my positive intention, and truly surrender to the outcome. It may work out or it may not, but I had to fully surrender to the notion that a higher purpose was working for me, and not against me.

So set your intention, establish your goal, and put the effort in, but then allow yourself to surrender to the outcome. Keep doing your absolute best and give yourself patience, time and kindness. If you hit an obstacle, acknowledge the emotions of pain, disappointment or hurt, but then use every fibre of your strength to let it go, let it fade away. Witness it as an observer. The obstacle was there, and you can't change that, so what can you do now to get back on track? What would be your advice to someone else in a similar position? Work on that, and redirect your energy towards it. Let the journey unfold and flow as it should without any force placed upon it. In a world where we want progress and answers yesterday, it may feel hard to surrender, but it's not impossible. It takes practice, but it's worth the time and effort. The journey may take a little longer and may take you on some unexpected paths and out of your comfort zone, but trust that it is all happening in your favour.

Letting things flow applies to all situations big and small. When you are standing in the queue and someone in front of you has a full trolley of items and numerous coins and coupons, instead of tutting or cursing at them in your mind or maybe even showing them your annoyance, try doing something productive. Maybe practise a little gratitude for the fact that you are in a supermarket with so much choice and variety to nourish you, with an abundance of items to meet your needs. It may be that you are in a warm, sheltered place and grateful for the ability to walk or get transport here and that your body and its mobility have allowed you to do this. Or focus on whatever else you are grateful for that day. Maybe you could send someone a text to check in on them, or practise a little breathwork. Getting annoyed isn't going to make the shopper move any faster or the till operator go any quicker. Use your time effectively, and who knows what magic will come from it?

Maybe that career goal is taking longer than you thought; keep putting the work in and trust that there is a higher purpose. You are growing in strength, patience, wisdom and knowledge, and when you get to where you need to be, it will be at the right time for you. I remember another time desperately wanting something, and for three years I was rejected for the role; however, when I did finally receive it, my mindset had grown stronger, and I wasn't reliant on it making me happy. I was grateful, and still loved being given the role, but my association with it had changed. I no longer felt that I would at last be happy once I received it; I was happy regardless, and that was an important place for me to get to; therefore, the role came at the right time for me. It may even be that the universe is guiding you to something better or something completely different that you may not even have considered; you will align with the reason when it happens.

I used to take everything personally when things went wrong, saying that those things only happened to me, that I always had bad luck, that it just had to rain today, that everyone else but me seemed to succeed, and so on. The longer I sat with those thoughts and that low energy, the more of them I seemed to attract to myself, and I would end up in a downward spiral.

The more you focus on certain areas, the more you notice them. This also stems from our subconscious wiring: the more you have the same thought pattern, the more that wiring becomes stronger, and therefore you notice even more frequently things that make you think problems only ever affect you. Ever wanted to go to a certain holiday destination or buy a certain car? Suddenly, you see that destination everywhere in various ways: friends are going there, you see adverts for it, etc. And now you see that model of car on the road all the time. These things were always there, but you've wired your brain to be more aware of them now. (Just like I'm always the one who notices spiders in my house first!)

So, going back to me taking things personally: I had programmed myself to see things this way, and therefore, my perception was different to somebody else's. I could have the same five setbacks as another person in the same period of time, but I would believe it was 'my luck', while the other person would simply look for a solution and reroute or trust that it wasn't meant to be right then. My energy and flow were not allowing me to move forward or progress. I was more focused on it all going wrong for me, and I almost refused to see any other option or direction. I often didn't try again; I used to give up. I would sit with my thoughts and confirm to myself over and over again that I was a failure and regurgitate all the other times I had failed. I was in 'stuck' mode, and something had to change: me.

Now, I choose to surrender and let things go. I can only do my best, work to the best of my knowledge and try as much as I can. That part of the deal never diminishes, but I now go into it accepting that things may not go my way, plans can change and I may need to look at alternative paths. And that's okay.

Again, this is not easy work, especially if you are currently having a setback, are in 'stuck' mode or a state of funk. It's not about snapping out of it; it's about looking at your situation and seeing how you can move forward from it. It may be easier to give up and not do anything, but is it making you feel happy?

Live every day with a purpose, and do everything you can to move one step forward. What can you control and what can't you control? Work on what you can control. What's causing you pain, and how can you move away from that? Uplift yourself with kind actions and motivating words; you will get there. Keep working, keep going, and avoid any pressure.

Acknowledge your emotions – but the ones that don't serve you don't need to stay within you. You will feel a great sense of peace and liberation as you watch them float by rather than hold you back.

Trust that the universe has its own timing and plan, that it is supporting you if you choose to allow it. Lean into the universe's energy; let the current flow through you, carry you and guide you forward. Don't force or resist it; simply by working towards it without any pressure, you will get to where you need to be.

So, take these few thoughts into account:

1. The world is not against you or conspiring against you;
2. Embrace setbacks you can't control, but know that you can control your response to them;
3. It's entirely in your power how you choose to move forward;
4. Have 100 per cent good intentions, but let go of any expectation;
5. Surrender to the outcome, and allow the universe to support you in the right way at the right time;
6. Give yourself praise and credit for having the courage to try each day;
7. When you feel any frustration, anger or worry rising, acknowledge it, observe it and do your very best

to let it fade, employing the simple yet powerful practice of taking some deep breaths. Refocus on your next steps, and always keep going;
8. Over time, continue to observe any thoughts that don't serve you, and watch them float past; don't give them your attention or any reason to stay;
9. Remember that other people do not have the power to limit your progress; move away from any toxicity because you have the power to do exactly that;
10. There is a whole alphabet left when plan A doesn't work.

Well-being exercise

Let's do some breathwork to release tension and get in touch with your flow state.

Find a comfortable position, ideally where you can be seated on the floor cross-legged. If that's not comfortable, sitting on a chair or standing is absolutely fine; your comfort is the most important thing.

Ensure your space is distraction-free, and just take a few moments to settle yourself in.

If it's possible, gently shrug your shoulders up and down three times, then roll your neck first clockwise then anticlockwise three times each; now stretch your fingers then curl them three times before gently placing your hands on your lap palms facing upwards.

Now gently close your eyes, start to let any external noises and any internal thoughts drift away, and focus simply on your breathing.

Begin to take some nice deep breaths in and out. As you breathe in, notice that your belly expands, and as you breathe out, notice it deflate again. Take lovely slow, deep breaths. Breathe right into your belly and then out again.

Your mind may have intrusive thoughts coming in, such as what you'll be having for dinner or your to-do list for tomorrow, and that's okay and very normal. Simply observe the thoughts, but give them no attention; focus back on your breathing, and over time and with practice, the thoughts will become less frequent. Don't judge yourself or feel frustrated if you struggle with concentration: everything takes practice, time and patience.

To deepen your practice, you can focus on counting your breaths in and out; so, as you inhale slowly count to four, hold your breath for a count of four and then exhale for four. Continue this for three minutes initially, and then you can add seconds or minutes at each practice. Every time you exhale, imagine you are breathing out any stress or tension. As you breathe in, you are inhaling love and peace.

A deeper breathwork is to inhale for four, hold for four and exhale for six, making your exhalation longer than your inhalation.

This breathwork practice every day can really help you feel at ease, allowing you to melt away the tension and feel peaceful and in tune with your goals and intentions.

Face it until you make it

Do you ever go through life knowing things need to change, but feeling as if you don't know where or how to start or whether it's even worth the effort? Instead of answering these questions, you avoid them. You bury your head in the sand and carry on, you hope for the best, or you falsely believe this is your destiny and something you have to put up with.

The changes you know you would love to make could include anything and everything from your characteristics, habits, behaviour and attitude to your personal relationships with people, career goals, social goals, etc. The list is endless.

Maybe you know you have a temper that flares easily, or you become easily irritated and you wish you could be calmer; maybe you are in a long-term relationship that is no longer serving you and you need to leave but are afraid to do so; maybe you've been in a career for a few years but have discovered a passion for something else and are at a crossroads; maybe people have always seen you dress in a certain way but you want to experiment with a new style and are afraid of the reaction of others; or maybe you want to try a new gym class but are afraid of being the 'beginner'.

All new and different things cause fear; our brain is wired to be tuned in to fear, and it will do anything it can to protect you from the cause of fear. New changes cause fear because they invite possible setbacks, hurt, embarrassment, pressure and the spectre of judgement. So, your brain tries to convince you to avoid change and holds you back; this is where you have to push past these thoughts and let your brain know that whatever the change brings, you are ready to deal with it.

You have to face the uncomfortable situation, face your fears, face the unknown, face your past and your present, and step out of your comfort zone to see the magic begin. Sometimes we are forced into taking first steps; for example, when you start a new job, you are naturally apprehensive on your first day, but once that's over, things become a little easier and a little more familiar. When there is no one external pushing us, we need to generate the force that drives us to make those changes from within ourselves. Starting with just one thought and one step is all it takes.

I know. Easier said than done, right? But you really have been doing exactly this for a lot of your life. Think back to how many changes you have already gone through and how much you've achieved because of these changes that you had the courage to make. You will have gone through times when everything went to plan and other times when it didn't, but you made it through, and you are stronger and smarter than ever. The journey will continue, and you will find your way.

Question yourself. Would you be happy being exactly where you are in one year's time or in five years' time? Would you be happy to settle, knowing you never tried to give it a go?

In my life, I've gone through many transition periods that were definitely daunting: some where I knew what I wanted to do but had no idea how to start, some where I knew how to start but was afraid to take the first step.

I'll share a couple with you. One was going into my career as an optometrist but having a real passion for psychology and being a well-being coach for others. I had finished my optometry degree and was already wanting to pursue this next path. I didn't know where to start, which courses to go on, how to set up a business and how to face judgement on why I wanted to do something so different when optometry should be enough. However, I took it step by step, super slowly, and over the coming years I studied, learnt, asked for a lot of help and eventually set up my well-being business.

I had a secure job with relatively low stress, and as much as I loved it and still do, I had other passions and ambitions – and that's okay to want to try other things. It doesn't always have to be this *or* that, it can be this *and* that, unless you choose otherwise. I know many people who have held secure jobs that paid well but decided to let it all go and follow their passions despite the many questions and the concerns of others. It is scary, it is daunting, and there are no guarantees of the outcome, but it's also exciting to simply know you are being courageous and trying.

I remember when, at the very start of my well-being career over ten years ago, I completed my life-coaching course. I had a vision but had no idea where to begin with it or how it would end up. I just knew I had to take things step by step. What was the easiest first step? What was the most manageable first step? For me, it was to set up a website, then, having had some flyers made and heavily pregnant, I would walk around neighbouring districts posting them.

I remember people at the time questioning why I was adding pressure to my life by venturing into a new business; it made me doubt myself at the time, but remember that other people's opinions are just that – their opinions! Don't let them discourage you or persuade you to give up; they don't always know best despite their good intentions. You are not there to prove them right or wrong, and you are not living to validate their expectations of you. This is your life, and you can only live it your way. If you feel alone in the process, look for supportive networking groups instead; there are so many online and in-person groups available now supporting like-minded people.

Another example concerns an aspect of my character. I struggled quite a bit with social and general anxiety, and so I found it difficult to do certain things like eating in front of other people, driving to unfamiliar places, meeting people in social settings, etc., and I came across as shy, quiet and not very sociable. I then found this difficult to deal with, so my home life would consist of releasing my hurt through tears, low moods or anger. My moods were always, and I mean always, up and down.

I thought this was just me, just the way I was born; I didn't understand at the time that there was a whole landscape of past experiences and beliefs that I had stored that was making me behave and feel that way. I had to face who I had become to change into who I wanted to be. This meant having support, having therapy, understanding my past and ultimately understanding myself.

I learnt to embrace my shyness instead of hating it; I learnt to embrace the fact that I wasn't super loud or bubbly, and that was okay; it didn't need to make me any less likeable or even less sociable. I had held a belief since childhood that bubbly, confident, talkative people were the ones everyone liked best, but this was simply a notion rather than a fact or any sort of truth. I learnt to be honest about my journey when I was feeling uncomfortable, for example, telling people that I wasn't a confident driver, and asking if we could meet somewhere where there was a parking area the size of a football stadium. My true friends supported me instead of judging me. It was refreshing not to hide who I was.

Over the years, I faced myself and embraced myself. Where I wanted to see change, I took steps to create the change; other areas I grew to love, and I accepted them as being a part of me, something that I didn't want to change to fit in with someone else's expectations.

A more light-hearted area that I wanted to change was my fear of trying new classes. I had always wanted to give spinning classes a go, but I was always afraid of my ability and what everyone else would think. Fear of judgement from others is what usually stops people in their tracks, and this was me.

In my mind, there were people in the class really going for it, giving it their all, making it look easy and effortless, and then there would be me, probably not following the right instructions, getting exhausted after ten minutes, fretting about what people behind me were thinking and wondering how I would survive the next twenty. I had built up such a story in my mind, but was it worth not trying a class because I was afraid of other people? Should I never give it a go? Well, for a good five years, that's exactly what I did. I didn't face it, and I continued to look in from the outside, wishing over and over that I could just go for it.

Then, as I began growing and strengthening my mind, I happened to go to somewhere where they offered spin, and I faced myself and again was honest about my journey. As I entered the spin class, I saw two other people already on their bikes. I gave a smile and went to a bike. When the instructor came and asked if anyone was new, I said I was new to spin and joked that I was very scared; those last four words then made people around me smile and open up. I heard encouraging words and friendly quips such as 'we aren't new, but we still get scared', or 'you'll love it' or 'just do what you can; you've shown up, and that's the hardest part', and this all made the process so much lighter, and I actually had a really fun – hard, but fun – class.

It really is liberating when you face yourself rather than avoiding yourself. The magic really does happen when you step outside of that comfort zone. When you practise becoming comfortable in your own skin, you stop worrying about trying to fit in with other people.

You have one shot at life and many opportunities to live it in different ways.

Take a moment to look at where you are right now. If you could be anything, wear anything, try anything, go anywhere, do anything, what would all that look like for you?

It's a HUGE question, so take your time; keep your mind absolutely open without the ifs and buts: if it was all available and possible what would your answer be?

Write it down.

I will give you some of my answers over the years:

- Wear a jumpsuit (always thought they looked cool but thought they wouldn't suit me);
- Wear red lipstick whenever I felt like it (worried what people thought);
- Set up a business (thought it might fail);
- Take a spin class (thought people would laugh at me secretly);

- Take up running (dreaded passers-by looking at me);
- Sit in a coffee shop on my own (worried people would wonder why I was alone).

These answers illustrate my lack of confidence and my concerns about what other people would think. I had to face myself, my confidence issues and my past; I had to work on this and then believe that I had just as much right to do any of those things, or at least try them, as anybody else. I didn't need others people's approval, applause or anything else, and whether my jumpsuit suited me or not or if I was terrible at spin class – who cared? I was doing it for me, and that was enough. I've transformed in so many ways by facing myself and continue to do so.

What to do next?

What do you need to do to take some small steps towards your objectives? It could be as simple as going into a clothes store and trying on a new look in the fitting room and maybe purchasing one outfit, and perhaps scheduling in a day when you would then wear the outfit.

Maybe you like how you dress but always feel conscious among other people, believing they are judging your appearance. Remind yourself that true friends love you for you and that you have the freedom to dress as you please; you certainly don't need to please other people.

You could do a simple Google search on some new courses you would like to try; maybe you could write a top-five list and then consider some pros and cons to help you select one. This could be the step into changing your career.

There may be parts of you that you felt you had to change to fit in but that you now actually embrace. If people have been making you feel a certain way, then maybe this is the time to slowly reduce contact with them and instead start connecting with those who make you feel good.

Ask a friend to join you at a new class you want to try, or maybe try the class at a quieter time so it builds your confidence.

Small, manageable steps are all you need to move forward. Don't think too much about the end result or outcome, as that can feel overwhelming. If I was thinking about the end goal of this book, it would feel like an enormous task, but if I were to think about simply the first page, and then the next, it would feel less daunting and more achievable.

Well-being exercise

One of my absolute favourite things to do is create a vision board; it's fun, it's uplifting, and it really allows the imagination to run wild.

Get a large sheet of paper or board, coloured pens and magazines of interest.

Think about everything you want to have, feel, see and experience in life. Go crazy with your thoughts and dreams, without thinking *But that won't ever happen* or *That's not possible*. Every small wish and every large dream can go on this vision board.

There are absolutely no rules when creating your board.

I always like to write an empowering message in the centre, such as 'ALL DREAMS ARE POSSIBLE', 'MY LIFE, MY WAY' or 'I WELCOME ABUNDANCE IN MY LIFE'; something in the present tense that resonates with me. Do this.

Then, cut out some images that reflect your dreams from the magazines you have chosen, or print some out from the internet. You might, for example, cut out an image of your dream home or your ideal holiday destination, career or hobby. Maybe you want to be a runner. Find a picture of a track or of yourself running. Or, if you want to visit a certain restaurant, find a picture of that restaurant. Maybe you want more family time; if so, find pictures of your family doing something fun.

Stick these images on your paper, and if you wish, you can add some words next to them – simple, empowering phrases such as 'family fun time', 'long walks in Scotland', 'sleeping under the stars', 'head of marketing at the Joe Bloggs company', 'scuba diving on the Great Barrier Reef', 'fitter and leaner', etc.

Whatever flows into your mind and onto the sheet, let it be; enjoy this and have fun with it.

Once your vision board is complete, place it somewhere you can see it regularly.

Allow your mind and intentions to work towards the words and images, and remember to focus on what you want and not what you don't want.

Forgiveness

A definition of the word 'forgive' is 'to stop feeling angry or resentful towards someone for an offence, a flaw or a mistake'.

When we don't forgive others, that generates strong emotions of anger, hurt and resentment. These emotions can really cause a lot of internal destruction, especially as we continue to layer on the feelings, adding further stories to the original emotions and letting ourselves get triggered again and again by the same people.

In our life, we will cross paths with many people and form varying relationships with them. We have family, friends, partners, colleagues, acquaintances and new people we continue to meet. Some of these people may cause us hurt intentionally or unintentionally at different levels and times. We may have a parent who never seems to show interest in our life or is always quick to judge or criticise; we may have other family members who go out of their way to exclude us or make us feel small; we may have friends who seem to always take but never give or only show up when they require something; we may have colleagues who don't show us the same respect as others or use us for their own benefit; and we may have partners who have betrayed our trust. Some of this hurt can last for extended periods of time, and we may try to understand those who have offended us, give them the benefit of the doubt or even make excuses for them.

Sometimes, the hurt can be in smaller measures but still have an impact on us. We might, for example, text someone who doesn't respond for days, even though we are always the first to make the effort to check in on people when those same people never take the initiative to check in on us; or we might consistently make kind gestures to those around us without ever receiving anything in return. The hurt felt lasts so much longer than the offending action, or lack of action. This hurt can also arrive in different phases.

First, we question ourselves and try to understand. We wonder if we have done something wrong. *Am I at fault? Is it because they don't like me? Did I not make enough effort or say the right things? Did I not come across as friendly, approachable or fun? Did I make a mistake or error of judgement somewhere? It must just be something about me* ... We are especially perplexed if we witness them giving what we desire to other people. This makes us feel low, and our self-worth and esteem drop. At this point, we may even try one more time with those people that are hurting us, in the hope that it may be different this time. One more text, one more gesture, one more form of effort and time invested in them. When the outcome is the same, this is when the next phase enters – resentment.

We start resenting these people who continue to hurt us, resenting the fact that they are oblivious to the pain they are causing us and the impact it is having on our emotional health. We want them to know and feel our pain, we want them to see and understand how their actions are making us feel, we want them to acknowledge it and be sorry. We also know that without confrontation, they may never understand, and our anger and frustration continue to bubble underneath the surface.

Subconsciously, we may even try and make known to them what we are feeling, maybe with a look, a cryptic text message or words in a conversation – something that isn't direct, but we hope they read between the lines and get the message.

Then, there are the larger, deeper hurts: when a partner betrays your trust, when you have been bullied, when family members insult you, when friends leave you out, when figures of authority wrong you somehow. These hurts penetrate more deeply because of the situation, the shock and the intensity of the feelings. These are incidents imprinted on your heart that you may still vividly remember five or ten or twenty-plus years later.

There are days when we can forget about it or be distracted from it, but when we are triggered again either by crossing paths with the person in question or by having some sort of interaction with them, the hurt resurfaces.

We live in this cycle of pain, questioning ourselves and moving from trying to understand through anger and frustration and back to hurt. We live in this unhealthy cycle unless we choose an alternative, and that is FORGIVENESS.

Forgiveness is consciously letting go of anger, hurt and resentment towards another individual. It doesn't mean you are condoning or excusing their behaviour but rather that you are choosing to no longer have an emotional response to them.

Even considering forgiving someone is a huge step; you can feel conflicted about the idea because it can make you feel that they have 'got away with it'. However, you have to ask yourself this: if you don't forgive them, who will the situation impact more, you or them? They are continuing with their life possibly unaware of the impact their actions are having on you, whereas you are still being consumed by hurt and frustration. Remember that everything is energy and that holding on to these feelings towards someone results in the lowering of our own vibration.

By forgiving them in your heart and mind you are actually choosing yourself over them. You are saying that their actions and words will no longer take up any more of your time or energy. By truly letting them go, you will experience a beautiful sense of freedom and peace.

I get it ... You are still hesitant, because by forgiving and moving on, you still have to accept the fact that they will never understand your pain and what they did. This is where you have to dig deep, have faith, and trust in the process.

The fact is that you really don't know their full story. They could have huge personal issues, past traumas, insecurities and hurts of their own, which cause them to behave the way they do towards you. They may have deep-rooted issues, they may simply not be aware of their actions, there may be multiple reasons, and there may not be any. These are not excuses but simply parts of the whole story. The truth is something you will never fully know. They are also not you, and so even if you think *but I would never say or do that* or *I would behave so differently*, you cannot expect another person to react in the same way as you. Let go of the ego when the self needs to be understood and soothed before it can move on; trust that making it right and finding peace from within will change the energy in and around you. You will realise how much space you had reserved in your mind for that person, and when it becomes free, you will feel a sense of relief: that person and their actions have no hold over your happiness.

People respond in so many ways, depending on their own past and experiences. Some people may not respond to text messages for days, because they are genuinely busy or they forget or they had intentions to reply but became distracted, while others will respond within seconds because they do have the time, or it's their habit to answer texts straight away or it's simply something they like to keep on top of.

Some family members won't give you their support or love in the way you would like for a number of reasons. Maybe they had a difficult upbringing and find it difficult to express emotions after having to suppress their own for such a long time. Maybe they have built a wall within them so as not to become too attached to others because of past rejections; maybe they are genuinely unaware of your needs or their actions; or maybe they are envious or jealous of you. Very often, their behaviour is due to a void within them. They may see parts of you as the missing parts of them – your job, your family life, your personality, your appearance, etc. There may be small triggers that cause them to treat you the way they do, almost as a form of defence or protection of themselves. They make a conscious and sometimes subtle effort to make you feel small or excluded … in order to make themselves feel better and elevated.

The reasons are endless, and even if you were to directly ask them why they behave the way they do, they might not tell you the full truth, because they may not fully understand it themselves. They may not be honest about their true reasons; they may not even realise they have wounds acquired in the past that have not been healed. They may deny the issue and become defensive, argue about it, think they did the best they could or genuinely be unaware of it. They may not change, instead expecting you to change, or their own healing process may be taking a long time.

You may perceive the situation to be very black and white where you are right and they are wrong. All the facts might support that view; they truly may be selfish, arrogant, disrespectful, uncaring, etc. Whoever they are and whatever they did, you cannot force them to be accountable, and you cannot force them to change. You can, however, now preserve your energy and boundaries; let this no longer be between you and them but instead between you and the universe. Stay true to yourself; stay peaceful, kind and humble; and don't let someone else's actions fill you with bitterness and resentment.

I'll gives you a couple of examples of when it was difficult to understand someone. I was working with a client aged thirty-five. They had a difficult upbringing where the father always appeared to favour the younger siblings, and he made this person's life very difficult. The father was abusive to the mum, and this client witnessed some awful things in his childhood. At the age of eighteen, when he left home to go to university, he cut ties with his father and didn't speak to him again. The parents were divorced at this stage. However, for his whole life, he had carried this hurt: he couldn't understand why his father didn't love him like a father should, why there was never any care or joy or happy father-and-son moments. He questioned over and over whether he had done something wrong, and this led to him having anxiety and low self-esteem. During our session, we worked on the fact that his childhood needs were never met; however, he was an adult now, and the questions without answers were no longer serving a purpose. His whole life was on hold, as he couldn't let go of the past and couldn't live for the present. It was important for him to understand that this thirty-five-year-old no longer needed his father's love, validation or praise; he didn't need him to feel secure or know his worth. As a child, he needed a father to love and support him, but that was then, and this is now. He was no longer that child, and everything he required he could provide for himself through his own agency. He could now validate, love and praise himself, and he was no longer dependent on anyone.

Again, this is initially a very difficult thing to do, as the brain likes to understand and make sense of the world in order to process events and move on. It's our job to retrain the mind and tell it that it's okay in this instance not to have the need to understand in order to move on. He had a conversation mentally, letting his father know that he was a total idiot and selfish and that his actions were a reflection of his own wounds, and that he, my client, no longer cared any more; he was living his life for himself now, and that in itself felt so liberating.

One period of my own life saw me finding fault in a certain person for many years. I would always see the hardship they imposed, the lack of effort in their words and actions. I almost kept looking for these traits to prove and confirm how 'not nice' they were. Later on down the line, as I did the inner work and began to let go, I realised they would never have met my expectations, because I had been hurt so much in the past by wounds that had not been healed, and they would therefore never do enough to fill my void. That was on me, and not their responsibility. I also realised that for them, just surviving day-to-day life was enough; that was all they could manage, let alone expending any extra effort or energy elsewhere. The little they were giving was all they had to give. However, I was so focused on my needs that I failed to see theirs, and even if I didn't understand them, it was my responsibility to let it go.

Because I was lonely and insecure and had very low self-esteem, my gestures were always over the top. I would go out of my way to do things, always sending messages to see how they were and sending treats every now and then, all in the hope that they would like me and fill this deep void I had.

They were never going to meet my expectations, because their needs were not the same as mine, and whatever they did give me was never going to be enough, because I would always crave more. My need to feel wanted and to belong was too big for any person to ever fill; however, I didn't realise this at the time, and I didn't realise the only person able to fill it was me.

I let them know on numerous occasions, directly and indirectly, how they made me feel, and the truth was I could never understand their responses. I always felt misunderstood … and in hindsight, I realised they felt the same. To me, it felt as if they didn't care enough and that to them, I was simply being too needy or wanted too much from them; perhaps they truly didn't realise anything was wrong.

Over time, I realised I would never receive what I had in mind, even though my expectations were minimal, because I was not them and they were not me; we would never fully understand each other. I was wrongly depending on other people for my happiness. There is not one person out there, including a partner, child or family member, that can be responsible for your happiness. Others can support it, add to it and be part of it, but they can never be the sole cause of it.

My past experiences of moving to different schools, not settling, always feeling like an outsider and not having a group of friends where I belonged had over time caused immense loneliness. I witnessed friendships around me, observing the joy and security it gave others not worrying about who your partner in PE would be, who you would sit next to at your desk, who you would sit on the bus with, who would invite you for a play date. All this felt like an elusive dream ... It was something I never had and something I longed for. I was forever trying to recreate those moments of what I had felt about the things I had missed out on with anyone that crossed my path over the years. I wanted them to fit in with the idealistic dream in my head.

Letting it go was the hardest yet the most incredible thing I did for myself, and one of the biggest steps I took in my healing journey. Letting go of needing people to be a certain way, letting go of my expectations, letting go of trying to understand, letting go of wanting their approval, letting go of them. I don't mean cutting ties off completely; I mean letting go of the mentally draining energy between us. I needed to let them live and be their own version of themselves and not my version, and I needed to begin to fill my own void.

You can trust that the universe has a phenomenal energy. It acknowledges when you release your negative energy and when you replace it with a positive, flowing one. When you choose to forgive, that is exactly what you are doing, and as you release, you are actually inviting an abundance of positivity to enter your life, including new people.

It's not an easy step, but it's certainly a courageous one, and this is where, if you take the conscious decision to forgive those people who are no longer serving a purpose in your life, you will be making one of your best decisions. When you forgive, you have to do everything in your power to mean it, to believe it and to feel it, and to genuinely let them go. I also appreciate it's harder to do with some people than others, such as a parent, of whom you would naturally have higher expectations. However, even a parent, if you strip away the title, is just a person with their own flaws and past wounds.

As an adult, you will ask questions about how a parent could 'do this' or 'make me feel this way' or 'treat me like that', and the same principles apply here. You will never fully understand them, and even if you think you do, it will still make you question why they acted as they did. They didn't get it; times were different then; they didn't realise; they had no choice; they had their own problems and hardships; they were just trying to do their best; etc. These are some of the many reasons I hear when I work with clients. It doesn't always help, and it still hurts, so acknowledging that you were hurt is where to start; processing it and understanding that you can't change it is the next step; and the final stage is working on letting it go and moving away from the pain towards peace.

This means not 'accidentally on purpose' dropping hints and giving subtle messages to those in question. This means not giving certain looks or using any other body language that could show your hurt or annoyance at them should they cross your path. To let go means really letting go. It won't be an overnight fix where your feelings disappear, but they will fade over time, and your need for that person to know or understand will have less importance in your life.

In a relationship where someone has caused hurt and betrayal, process the situation, but then begin to clear up the negative energies that you are holding on to. Questions about why they did that, why you deserved it and how they could break your home and your trust, along with replaying conversations and actions, will serve no long-term purpose. Forgive, and wish them well in your heart; trust that this was not the right person for you and that possible past karmic consequences brought your paths together. This can be very hard where children are involved and where you may have to face your partner regularly, or if the partner isn't being there enough, or at all, for your children. Keep striving to change any hate, hurt and resentment towards them to love, peace and hope for yourself and your journey forwards. Remember that forgiving them means choosing YOU over them.

Letting go can mean distancing yourself as much as possible from that person or simply having minimal contact, if any. Peacefully accept this period of your life and their role in it, and now reset for the future ahead. We are all souls on a temporary journey on this earth; let them carry on with theirs and you with yours.

Take a moment to think about the people that have caused you hurt. Make a choice today to let them be and let them go. They played a purpose in your life, maybe to show you how strong and resilient you are or to show you that you can rise above hard situations and that you have to go through the toughest experiences to get to a better place.

Before my ex-boyfriend broke up with me, we had chosen to do the same course at the same university three hours away from home. I would never have chosen that university and probably not that course either if it hadn't been for him. However, being on that course at that university eventually led me to my husband, my family and a career I love. We may not see it at the time, but trust that there really is a higher purpose.

People in your life are a test to show that actually you do matter as a person, that you are worthy of kindness and love, that you don't need people to depend on for anything including your happiness, that you can more than cope without them and that love starts from within you. Feel that hurt and anger melt within you and be replaced by a flow of love for yourself as you make that decision to choose YOU.

Expecting the world to be our version of perfect

We want life to be perfect, we want people in our lives to be perfect, we want situations to be perfect, we want our bodies to be perfect, we want our homes to be perfect, we want our place of work to be perfect, and we want that definition of perfect to be our version of perfect.

We want what perfect means to us based on our past, our beliefs and our expectations. Yet despite learning through experience that perfection doesn't exist, we still desire it. We will always find fault; we will always see the imperfections; and we will always question and wonder why something or someone isn't fitting in with our world.

Why is that person speaking to me like that? Why are my children never as tidy or as organised as me? Why does my husband not understand me? Why do my parents and in-laws never appreciate me? Why does my boss always cause me anxiety? The common word in all these scenarios is 'me'. Why are they not fitting in with 'me' and my idea of perfection?

Is your way really the best way, the right way? Says who? Others also have the right to ask why you are not fitting in with them, don't they? We spend so much time and energy wishing and hoping that other people will change, but how much time do we spend trying to work on ourselves instead?

You have a choice to accept people for who they are, or, if they are impacting you and your life in such a way that you are struggling, either step away or create changes within yourself. The world is very much perfectly imperfect, and we either need to make compromises or accept that we want something different from what we are getting and do something about that.

In a household setting where you live with each other, you have to communicate, understand and compromise, talking to your family members but also listening. It should never be 'I am right and you are wrong', no matter how obvious a situation may seem. Come to a solution or compromise together, finding something you can all agree on. I always perceive my family as a jigsaw puzzle; we are four individual, unique pieces, but each brings a different benefit when we're joined together. Sometimes, finding compromise can be difficult; for example, if you live with in-laws, you may need to create boundaries to protect your space.

Accepting that you cannot change anyone else is the first step; however, you can change yourself and create healthy boundaries, or you can move away from them.

Sometimes our version of wanting perfection means having a respectable, nurturing environment, and so if, for example, a colleague's behaviour renders your place of work toxic, you might begin to look for employment elsewhere. It may seem daunting, but it is possible and may be the step you need to take. If you decide to stay, remember this is a choice; you can discuss the issue with the person in question, but if nothing changes, you will have to alter your own mindset and focus on your work, creating your own calm working environment and reducing contact with the person impacting you. There are always options and choices, such as speaking to HR, your union, mediators or other professionals; doing this may put you out of your comfort zone, and it may seem easier to simply put up with the situation, but is that what you really want for your future?

I have been in a work situation where a colleague consistently upset me. I spoke to them; they felt they were not doing anything wrong and that I was being too sensitive. I began to reduce any contact with them unless absolutely necessary and just focused on my role; however, over time, I realised I wasn't enjoying going to work, and even though my job was familiar and comfortable with an easy commute, etc., it still wasn't enough when I was feeling anxious daily. I chose to move: it felt scary, unfamiliar and uncertain, but it was the best decision I ever made. Sometimes these situations arise because the universe has a higher plan for you.

People often feel stuck because they feel unable to leave certain people or situations: a work place that you have been in for numerous years, family members to whom you are bound biologically or through your marriage or your partner, friendships that you've had for years. I want to tell you, really emphasise to you, that YOU CAN LEAVE anyone and anywhere. The only ties are the ones you have created in your mind.

It may not be easy, but is what you are going through right now easy? No. It's just become familiar, and so you continue to take it. Our brain makes us feel there are limits and restrictions to what we can do; it likes to do what feels familiar, comfortable and easy. We have to constantly remind ourselves that we can reach further, we can go beyond familiar, we can go above what is the normal, we can do absolutely anything we want: it's OUR CHOICE, and we can make anything new and different familiar over time. We never have to put up with anyone or anything that doesn't make us feel good in any way; their role as manager, sister, father-in-law, best friend, etc., should never ever give them any power over you.

Let us look at another aspect of what perfection means to us, and where our version of it may have stemmed from. Often, our perception of 'perfect' is what we see of other people's lives. Their 'perfect' relationship, home, friendship groups, appearance, career success, etc. They look happy, they look like they have it all, they know what they are doing – and so we assume that's what we too must need for happiness: to feel the same as they are … or appear to be.

What we 'see' or 'hear' is not everything but simply a highlight in a social-media post, a story, a text message or maybe even a brief conversation. We add our own stories to those pictures and words and create many assumptions. They are lucky, they have it all, they are where we want to be, they have it easy, they have supportive people around them and the right contacts, etc.

When you think these thoughts, remember to question everything. Look deeper and beyond, and remind yourself there's more to the outcome than what we see on the surface. People feel more vulnerable if they show all the ups and downs that lead to the highlights. Being judged, being disliked, being seen as a failure: these are reasons why people don't want to show you the struggles they have encountered.

How many hours of work were done, how much stress and angst was endured, how many setbacks or sacrifices were encountered before the picture of the dream home appeared? How many rejections, how many late nights, how many courses before the dream job was achieved? It's not about the negatives; it's about looking at the reality of the whole picture. There is always more to it than meets the eye.

Every individual deserves happiness, so when you see someone experiencing a moment of theirs, send them love and good wishes. Remember the hard work they have gone through to get there, and remember that their story is still going on, as is yours. Their happiness shouldn't influence your own.

When you look at celebrities and influencers living their best life, remember that they too are going through their own struggles. The larger the platform, the greater the judgement they face and the harder they have to work on strengthening their mindset. It doesn't matter where you are or what stage you are at; everyone is on a journey. Focus on yours, and give compassion and good wishes to others.

The chances are that you will always be chasing your perfect home, appearance, car, gadget, etc., unless you start to focus on the happiness that lies within. You may have achieved some of the things that you feel happy about, but do you still sit there and think *if only my house had one extra bedroom*, or *I love my home, but wouldn't it be great if the garden was a little bigger or if we had a walk-in wardrobe?* Maybe you go on a dream holiday, but you wish the sea was calmer, the weather a little warmer or the service friendlier; or perhaps it's so good you wish you had an extra day or two. You look at your appearance, and you feel good until you look at someone on social media; then you wish that your hair was longer or your figure leaner, that you were taller or shorter, or that you had that beautiful outfit, etc. You believe that having any of these things will make you happier than you are. We want things to make our lives more 'perfect', and when we get the things we thought would do just that, we are left wanting more of them or even something else.

Maybe your version of 'perfect' stems from what you were conditioned to believe as a child. You may have heard your parents speak about the 'perfect partner' or the 'perfect house' and you've grown up having the perception that they described.

Perfection doesn't exist, and so chasing it won't make you happier; it will merely give you a false sense of hope that ephemeral things equal happiness. When you have had your 'perfect' job, phone, home, clothes, date night, holiday, etc., has it given you enduring happiness? Maybe it made you feel good, but how long did that last? Are you still in that exact same blissful state now that you were then? No – because now you want something else ... and you've told yourself you will be happy when you get that. Rather than adding meaning to your life, you try to recreate past moments that have brought you happiness. Do you ever reminisce about how happy you felt on your wedding day or when you got the job promotion or had that epic celebration party or enjoyed a phenomenal holiday? Do you say 'the happiest day of my life was when ...'? Do you wish you could relive that moment all over again? If so, why? It's because you are still chasing happiness, reaching into the future but also into your past. Happiness lies in the present, within you, right now. Happiness isn't out there, dependent on something external to you; it really is inside of you. Happiness is available to you right now, and inner happiness will never be impacted by, or dependent on, external factors.

Well-being exercises

Exercise 1

Write down the names of three people you compare yourself with (in terms of lifestyle, appearance, profession, etc.).

For each person:

- Write down three things that they have achieved;
- Write down against those three things what you think the person would have had to do to achieve them;
- Write down three possible challenges they may have experienced along the journey.
- Now write down three things that this person has done that inspire you.

Now repeat the following three times:

- I wish this person well; they deserve love, happiness and success.

Exercise 2

Write down a list of three people from whom you would like change (e.g. a mean boss).

Write down the changes you would wish to see from them (e.g. I want them to be nicer to me).

Write down why you want these changes (e.g. to feel valued and appreciated).

Do these changes reflect your idea of 'perfect'?

Write down three ways you can start changing and adapting instead (e.g. speak about my feelings in case the person is unaware, value and praise myself, look for progression elsewhere).

Change your perception and you'll change your world.

Imposter syndrome

I know when I say the words 'imposter syndrome', you know EXACTLY what I mean, right?

You know, it's that feeling where you question whether you are capable of doing a certain role. Is it really you that can do the task? Surely there is someone better out there with more skills, more knowledge, more experience. In fact, about ten people spring to mind in an instant. Maybe your boss has made a mistake. Maybe it is one of those ten that was meant to actually be doing this role. This promotion surely can't be meant for you; you still don't know enough, you're not up to it. Everyone will soon realise it was a giant mistake …

You're starting a new venture, and you're getting the customers or clients, but the doubts creep in. There are so many other people doing exactly what you are doing; they're so much bigger and more established than you. You can't possibly be as good as them, can you? There must be smarter, wiser, cleverer people than you. What if you let your customers down?

Imposter syndrome causes you to doubt yourself, your achievements, your talents and your ability and have a constant fear of being seen as a 'fraud'. It essentially comes down to believing you are not good enough and that you don't deserve your success or your accomplishments or the role that you are in. These beliefs can stem from past experiences from childhood onwards and are expressed in traits including anxiety and low confidence and self-esteem.

Imposter syndrome can be managed by understanding the power of thoughts and separating facts from beliefs. When certain thoughts that question your ability arise, instead of engaging in the conversation, simply observe the question, and if it doesn't help you, then let it go. If your mind doesn't want to let it go, then begin to reframe the mindset: you can respond and say, 'I am absolutely capable of doing this task, and I am excited to learn anything I may not understand and to grow. I am just as worthy as anyone else in giving this opportunity a go. I am committed and dedicated to making this work, and will do what it takes to move forward.'

Asking for support, not understanding something and then finding a way to learn about it, filling gaps in your knowledge, etc. are not signs of being less than capable; they demonstrate a growth mindset where you are continuing to build upon what you already know and becoming even better at your role.

Every single person starts from somewhere; no one is an overnight expert in their field, and even the most talented and successful people continue to learn and grow every day.

There are several different types of imposter syndrome:

Perfectionist

This type of imposter syndrome occurs in individuals who set excessively high standards for themselves and feel like frauds or failures if they fall short of those standards. They often believe that any mistake or imperfection is a reflection of their incompetence; this leads to constant self-criticism and fear of being exposed.

Superwoman/Superman

This type involves individuals who feel the need to work exceptionally hard and accomplish everything on their own. They often believe that their success is solely due to their intense efforts and that they must maintain high levels of productivity at all times. As a result, they may struggle to ask for help or delegate tasks, fearing that this would reveal their perceived inadequacy.

Natural genius

Those with the natural genius subtype believe that their worth is solely based on their ability to excel effortlessly. They feel pressure to quickly grasp new concepts and skills without much effort. They may become anxious or discouraged when they encounter challenges or when they need to put in significant effort to achieve their goals.

Soloist

Soloist imposter syndrome occurs when individuals feel they must accomplish tasks entirely on their own to prove their competence. They may hesitate to seek assistance, fearing that asking for help would expose their lack of knowledge or ability. This can lead to feelings of being isolated and overwhelmed.

Expert

Expert imposter syndrome is seen in individuals who constantly feel the need to acquire more knowledge or qualifications before considering themselves competent. They downplay their expertise and believe that they must possess an exhaustive level of knowledge before they can truly be considered competent in their field.

It's important to note that these subtypes are not mutually exclusive, and individuals may experience a combination of them or different subtypes at different times. Recognising the specific subtype of imposter syndrome you may be experiencing can help you understand and address the underlying beliefs and thought patterns contributing to your feelings of inadequacy.

Whichever one you resonate with, it doesn't need to define you, and it doesn't need to hold you back. It's important to understand what you are feeling, and it's important to know where those feelings may stem from, but it's also important to know that your situation can be managed and reframed.

Think about all the things you have already achieved.

We are often quick to think about what we haven't achieved or what we could do better; it's important to remember how far you have come. Think about all your skills and the characteristics that have got you to where you are now: the training you have done; other skills you have learnt; your resilience, kindness and openness to learning; your timekeeping; your organisation, listening and communication; your determination and drive; and all the other things you will have done. Don't hold back, because you really have done and achieved a lot.

When you notice imposter syndrome kick in, think about how much you have achieved; think about the times when you were unsure but learnt and developed in order to succeed in whatever task was at hand. Be assured that you care and that you aren't complacent; you want to be the best and deliver the best, and that's a good ambition to have.

It's okay to learn on the go, make errors, try again and find new ways to get to where you need to be. Even the most successful people have struggled to make every venture a winner. They may have achieved great things in one area and then tried something new that wasn't as good as they imagined it would be; however, instead of giving up, they found a different route to further success.

As I write this, I will in a few weeks be delivering one of my biggest presentations to date; the imposter syndrome does creep in at times, but I remind myself that first and foremost, I absolutely love what I do, I give it my absolute best, and I work very hard in delivering to the best of my ability. That is all I can do; if it goes well, that's fantastic, and if it doesn't, I will take the feedback and improve. I won't give up. I have been doing similar workshops for years, but every time they get bigger, the experience feels new again – but that's okay, because I am growing and learning as I go on.

It really is about making the unfamiliar familiar each and every time you do something new. Every time you do this, you continue to grow in confidence and knowledge and adapt to new ways. Remember that you are not an imposter; you are deserving of your role and your success.

Well-being exercise

I want you to find a picture of yourself and stick it in the middle of a sheet of A4 paper. Around it, I want you to put some arrows and add in writing all the things that you have achieved over the years.

You have already achieved so much, and it's important to remind yourself of this.

Some suggestions:

- When you started a new job
- When you did a presentation
- When you started a hobby
- When you learnt to cook
- When you supported someone
- When you listened to someone
- When you learnt to walk or talk
- When you took a test
- When you tried something new
- When you went to school
- When you stepped outside your comfort zone
- When you learnt a new skill
- When you tried again after a setback

Put this somewhere as a reference and a reminder for when imposter syndrome kicks in.

Why me?

Do you ever sit and look at your life, your situation, your circumstances, your struggles and your setbacks and think to yourself *Why me?* When the day doesn't go to plan, you spill your coffee, you can't find a parking space or you forget an appointment, do you think *Why me?* When people are rude to you or plans that you were excited about get cancelled, or when something happens that affects your health or you receive bad news, do you wonder *Why me?* You know that you should feel grateful for what you do have because there are people worse off than you, like the homeless or those living in poverty, but those thoughts make you feel even more guilty because you still think *Why me?*

I want you to know that it is absolutely okay to think *Why me?* It's a natural thought process to have. We are often impressed by other people's lives and believe things run smoothly for them; we see their outer image but don't often hear of their struggles or setbacks. We may see our colleague at work getting on with things, but we don't hear about the huge argument they had with their partner the night before. We see the parent on the school run with not a hair out of place, but don't see that she was up at 5 a.m. with her restless child and is absolutely shattered and that getting dressed and doing her hair made her feel better. We may see other people going out, having fun, etc. in the pictures they post but fail to see any of their life behind the camera: the overdraft they are worrying about when they go out, the break-up they are going through, the family traumas they have been living with.

So, if your question *Why me?* is enhanced by looking at other people's 'smooth' lives, remember and be mindful that you are never seeing the whole story and that they also may be thinking *Why me?* Thinking about other people will serve no purpose in your own path and life; it won't change your situation, and so it is better to reserve that time and energy for your own progress and your own path. So, what to do if you keep wondering *Why me?* or *When will things go right for me?*

Start with you, and you begin by changing the narrative. You are creating a story in your mind and painting an image that shows an individual almost in victim mode, where things small and large continue to go wrong for you. I recognise that you may get a little defensive here and say that things *do* keep going wrong. Yes, maybe they do. But can you do something about your misfortune instead of letting it be the final outcome?

Could you maybe change the story and reframe it

so that the things that have gone wrong can become a learning curve or growth pattern? Maybe the setback is a test of your character or a way for you to learn something different or new. For example, that thing that went wrong at work: instead of giving up or writing it off, maybe you can see this as an opportunity to learn a new skill, show off your knowledge and wisdom by finding a new path, or explore plan B or plan C.

Maybe you have just ended a relationship, and you are wondering why you can't seem to find the right one when everyone else seems to be happy and settled in great relationships. Break-ups are tough, but if it wasn't going in the right direction for you or them or both of you, then this was the right choice. It will be hard initially to adjust to a new normal; there will be emotional triggers and moments when you feel lost, but use the time to work on yourself. What is it that you need now? What will give you some joy and peace in this moment? A partner doesn't make you whole or complete; you were already whole without them – use this time to remember that. Rediscover who you are and your own identity; work on you; and trust that when the time is right, the right person will enter your life.

If you just can't seem to move forward in your career, instead of continually thinking *Why can I never progress when everyone else seems to?* do everything in your power to make a change. There is always something more you can do. Have you asked for support or feedback? Have you reached out to every contact in your network? Have you looked at further training? Have you looked at any personal blocks holding you back from doing any of these things and more?

Maybe you have ongoing health issues. It can be physically draining, and mentally draining too, continually wondering why you have a health-related problem, especially if you have been looking after your health and your illness has come out of the blue. Mindset is essential here: the primary focus needs to be loving your body, nurturing it and nourishing it. Prioritise your energy for self-love and self-care. Your body is your home, so yes, something may be happening to it, but continue to look after it so that, in return, it can continue to do its very best for you. You are your priority; rest, heal, be patient with yourself and take things one day at a time as you go through any changes. It can be hard seeing your body go through changes and maybe not being able to do things you once could, but continue to show yourself love and care.

As well as changing your story, change your actions. For example, if you know you are always frustrated at the weekly Saturday shop in the supermarket, why not change the day and time you go? The chances are it will be busy and crowded if you are going at the peak time with everyone trying to get their shop done in record time, so how about going very early or very late on a completely different day? Adjust your days and plans. It may feel strange at first, but you could see a huge improvement in your mood and you may actually enjoy the shopping experience.

Similarly, consider your routine car journeys. If there

is heavy traffic every day at the time when you need to be on the road, you could perhaps set off five or ten minutes earlier. It may seem impossible – trust me, I understand the challenge of trying to get two children, bags, packed lunches, etc. out of the house on time. To suggest getting away earlier seems impossible ... but it's not. Go to sleep earlier and set your alarm earlier; if you arrive early at your destination, do something fun or productive. When I arrive early on the school run, we sit in the car playing Would You Rather. It's a fun start to the day rather than a stressed and grumpy one, that's for sure.

When you start viewing and perceiving the world differently, you begin to respond to it much more peacefully. Happiness and the ebb and flow of life are never linear; there are ups and downs, but your response to your challenges determines how smooth those bumps feel. Your thoughts really can change absolutely everything.

Just like you, I have encountered endless setbacks, some bigger than others. Years ago, when I didn't value myself, when I didn't believe I was worthy, the setbacks felt like a confirmation to me. I believed it was the world's way of saying 'you aren't good enough, so I may as well make you feel that way by continuing to throw setbacks at you'. This would sadden and consume me, and a downward spiralling of my mood would ensue. An isolated setback would lead to me not feeling good for days and weeks, and my impression in those subsequent days would be that everything was going wrong. A trivial incident such as dropping my shopping would make me feel the world was against me; it would change my mood and emotions negatively, and because of my mindset, the rest of the day would be unproductive. As the day would be unproductive, I would feel as if further things were going wrong, when really my mindset had created that outcome.

When I began doing the inner work and realised that 'life happens' to everyone, from dropped shopping bags to deep break-ups, I stopped taking it all so personally. When I experienced a setback, the blow stopped feeling so heavy, I was able to accept and process it, and then I was able to recover and reset with the next plan. Dropped some shopping? Okay. Pick it up and move on without attaching stories and emotions to it. A rude customer experience? Okay. That person is obviously having their own struggles and not feeling happy; it's NOT because they don't like you or because you aren't good enough. When a friend would cancel plans on me at the last minute, I would think it was because I wasn't worth the time or they didn't like me, not because they simply couldn't make it for whatever the actual reason was. Maybe they were tired or something had come up or they weren't well: these would be the facts; however, I saw them as spurious reasons or excuses for the real reason – they simply didn't want to spend time with me. Again, this was all to do with my own limiting beliefs and past wounds and not about my friends. Later on, when someone cancelled on me, I took it as simply that: they cancelled, and that was that. No emotion or story attached ... apart from 'Damn, I was looking forward to that pizza!'

I used to always think that my husband was so lucky, that things flowed easily and effortlessly for him, that everything went his way all the time. I was blinded by tunnel vision and kept comparing my luck with his; but as I began to transform my own mindset, I realised it was HIS mindset and the way he responded to the world that made things flow. He chose to see the positives, to learn, to grow and to be grateful despite the challenges. It wasn't that he didn't have any setbacks; it was how he saw those setbacks and what he did with them that mattered.

It takes effort to practise this way of thinking, but the more you practise, the more it will come naturally. So, next time something doesn't go to plan or you have some bad news, see the event as an observer, and don't get attached to it or consumed by it. Step back, and really see the facts of the situation without attaching emotions and stories to it. Use the facts only to either let go of the moment or move forward productively.

Someone is unkind or you get delayed or you trip over: these things can be merely factual, and you can let go of them and move forward. The unkind person may have issues of their own, so wish them well; a delay has occurred, so use the waiting time productively; falling over was an unfortunate incident, so check yourself over and continue to move on with the day. Keep deleting the emotions and stories that aren't serving you; you don't need to hold on to them.

With something deeper, like receiving bad health news or not getting that job promotion, then of course process the information; your feelings are all valid. But then look at the situation factually to help you move forward. What do you need to do now to progress, to get better and to make positive changes? Answering this question can feel painful, emotional and hurtful, but being consumed by those feelings won't support or serve you in the long run. I'm not saying you should ignore the feelings; acknowledge and process them. You can say things about how the situation has made you feel sad, scared, nervous, unsure, etc., but then follow that by reminding yourself that it's okay to feel these things, but that you are now going to take practical steps. And note that a practical step could simply mean just taking a day to consciously rest.

These things may be happening in your life, but not because the world is out to get you. It is so important to try and release the fears and anxieties attached to events, allowing your energy to still flow and letting everything in your being feel loved and supported, no matter what might have happened. No progress is ever achieved by blaming others, blaming events or blaming ourselves.

Life happens to everyone, but it's how you perceive it and respond to it that matters, so give yourself the biggest possible chance of living a happier, more peaceful life. When you continue to work on yourself, when you continue to believe in yourself and to love and care for yourself, your happiness from within will grow and your perception of the external world will be more peaceful and joyful.

Well-being exercise

1. Note down three moments when you have wondered *Why me?*

What thoughts can you begin to change? (E.g. *Why do I never get a promotion?* can become *It's okay, the perfect promotion will come when the time is right for me. Right now, the time was better suited to the other person.*)

2. What positive actions can you take? (I will request feedback and support to find out if there is anything more that I can do to progress.)
3. What affirmation could be useful for each point? (I am learning and progressing daily, and my time is coming.)

As you begin to change your inner thoughts and world, your outer world will change too.

Being enough

First of all, I want to remind you that you ARE good enough exactly as you are right now; however, speaking from experience, I know that someone telling you that isn't always enough. The only way to feel enough is to believe it from deep within, and I want to get you started on that journey.

So many of our anxieties, fears and worries stem from our belief that we are not enough. However, if you are trying your very best with everything you have, then it truly is a just belief and not a fact, because everything you do and are *is* enough.

First, begin to question where this belief began: where in the timeline of your life were you made to feel you were not enough? There may be multiple areas that you can think of, some obvious and some not, but you were certainly not born feeling not good enough. This belief was created by the experiences you faced over the years.

Our brain is a complex and wonderful organ; its primary role is always to protect us emotionally and physically, but it can often get things wrong. Our subconscious mind stores all our experiences from birth up to where we are now: our memories, our milestones, everything we have heard and seen including the good and the bad – nothing gets edited or deleted.

Some of our negative experiences have a stronger hold because of the impact they had and the hurt and pain they may have caused, and so those times may be more vivid in our memory. If another event that causes a similar emotion happens, then this experience, and its associated feelings and beliefs, becomes stronger in the mind. Let me give you an example. As a child, when you appeared on stage at school in a production and forgot some of your lines because of nerves, you felt embarrassed and believed that you weren't good enough; your teacher was disappointed, and the other children were laughing. Later on, you avoided any public speaking; however, in a job interview, you had to give a public presentation, and the memory of your childhood came back to you reminding you how it made you feel. You began to feel anxious, flustered and nervous, and the presentation wasn't the best it could have been. This second event, which caused the same feelings of embarrassment, anxiety and not feeling good enough, is layered onto the first event. Now, any thought of public speaking will cause immense anxiety and fear because of previous experiences; your belief system is telling you that you can't do something, and its assertion is based on experiences from your past.

You can reprogramme these thoughts, you can change your beliefs, you can start to feel worthy and enough. Practise every single day being your own cheerleader. Root for yourself, high-five yourself, praise yourself, and keep encouraging yourself like no other. Take some public speaking courses, work on your presentation skills, keep doing presentations, look for ways to increase your confidence, ask for feedback, etc. Keep putting the work in, and over time, you will begin to notice a new belief system developing, one that says: 'I can do this'.

Take a moment to write down what it is that makes you feel you aren't good enough. It's important to be really honest with yourself here. Is it because you feel you aren't succeeding in a certain area? Are you comparing yourself with other people? Has something in your timeline made you feel this way? Or is it because of how other people are making you feel? If you don't know, ask yourself what it would be if you did know the answer. Whatever you feel is perfectly okay, but if it's not serving any purpose for you, then we need to find a positive way to process events and move forward.

Often, when we haven't felt valued or appreciated in our life, this can lead us to feel unworthy, and not enough. A full-time mum who has a lot to do every single day may not always feel valued by her children, or by her family members, and yet she continues to put the love and work in. A nurse may work long hours and never hear the words 'thank you' from her patients, and her manager may be too busy to praise or acknowledge her. Over time, this can lead to feelings of sadness and emptiness. A teacher, on the other hand, may have tough and challenging days, but may receive gifts at the end of the year, praise from colleagues, and support from the headteacher. They will thus feel valued at certain times. The mum in the previous example may not feel daily motivation or receive validation, but she could take steps to support her efforts to feel good enough by rewarding and praising herself and perhaps also meeting up with fellow parents, sharing thoughts and feelings and being in a space where people can boost and uplift one other.

If your feeling of not being enough relates to not achieving a goal or not getting there quickly, remember that results or progress don't determine whether you are enough. They simply show that a new path or direction is required: a reset. It's very normal to encounter challenges and setbacks and not get the expected results at the first or even the hundredth attempt. The greatest athletes and entrepreneurs, those who are the best in their field, will all have experienced what you are experiencing. Their problem wasn't not being enough, just as it's not your problem. They simply needed a change, a different plan, another perspective or even renewed perseverance.

People's words or actions don't make it true that you are not enough. Don't give other people permission to make you feel a certain way. That teacher who, when you were a child, made you lose your confidence; the parent who didn't show you love or praise you; that sibling or friend who never checks in with you or responds to you; the boss who doesn't give you the time of day: all of these people are influenced by their own issues; nothing of what they do or say reflects on you. Just let your mind sit with that for a moment.

Allowing others to dictate your worth gives them control over your mind and life. Take that control back. Those past experiences are not welcome in your present life, so let's work on developing that confidence and giving yourself that well-deserved praise. The inner child may still be searching for that approval, but you are an adult now, and you can absolutely validate and praise yourself; you don't need anyone to do this for you.

It is of course nice to get praise, but don't become dependent on it or have it as a requirement to know that you are doing okay. When we become reliant on it, it often becomes an addiction, and we continually need that next fix of validation.

For example, you might achieve something and people congratulate you. It feels good, you feel good, and you live off that adrenaline until it fades; then, you achieve something else, and you wait in anticipation of everyone congratulating or praising you once again, but no one comments or says too much this time. You begin to doubt yourself and your abilities; you question whether you are doing enough … all because of the absence of praise from other people.

It is so important to validate and celebrate yourself. Celebrate the positive difference you may be making to someone or something else, and don't let negative or indifferent feedback determine your happiness. Through the ups and downs, through the amazing things you do and give, let the validation that matters come from YOU. As your confidence and self-worth increase, so will your belief that YOU ARE ENOUGH.

It's not easy. I absolutely get it. It will take work, and it will take practice, but it really needs to be part of your inner process in order for you to live your life in peace and at ease.

You are enough when:

- You are winning at life AND when you experience setbacks;
- You know what you are doing AND when you really don't have a clue;
- You change your mind over and over;
- You feel good AND when you feel low;
- You get things right AND when you get things wrong;
- Other people appear to be way ahead of you;
- You are giving and not receiving anything back;
- You are making a difference without hearing the words 'thank you';
- YOU say you are.

You may not hear the words that you desire from others telling you that you are doing well, that you are appreciated, that they are proud of you and want to congratulate you. You may not receive awards, trophies or medals recognising your abilities and talents. Again, it's nice to have recognition from others; we are always looking for it. Even when someone wins a raffle or a game in the arcade or a bingo game on holiday, they feel a huge rush of happiness and excitement because an external win makes them feel good enough in that moment: something 'nice' happened to them; they achieved something good and were recognised for it. You may even hear people say 'I've never won anything before'; winning to them means something nice happening to them. But you don't need this type of external validation; if you are content inside, you are winning every day.

What you do have is the inner knowledge, the insider information, the truth from your heart and soul that you are giving it your all and trying your absolute best. Allow everything to start from that, then over time, you will see that any external praise is like icing on the cake; it's an extra bonus. It's nice but not necessary. Remind yourself every single day in every possible way that YOU ARE ENOUGH.

It's easy to stay stuck in the same thought patterns, telling yourself daily that you are not enough as a means of explaining why things don't go to plan. Perhaps you didn't get that job or a certain person didn't acknowledge you. You tell yourself that's okay and that it's because you are not enough and therefore shouldn't expect anything good to come to you. You continue with these low levels of expectation from the world and the people around you.

Now is the time to stop living life at a mediocre level; now is the time to fight back and begin to fulfil those dreams and wishes – because you are enough. You always have been.

Take some time to look back at situations that didn't make you feel good or people who didn't support or encourage you. Now, mentally tell them that they will no longer define you; they will no longer hold you back or have control over you. Whatever age you are, whatever stage in life you are at, it is never too late to change the noises in your mind from echoes of not being worthy to a proclamation of I AM ENOUGH.

You have a right to speak up for yourself, to chase your dream, to try again and again, to fall in love, to travel the world, to say no to things. You deserve all those things and more because you are worthy, but remember that who you are and where you are right now is more than enough too. You have always been enough, you are still enough, and when you continue to move forward in life you will be enough through the whole journey.

Well-being exercise

Get some colourful Post-it notes.

Write on each Post-it note the words 'I AM ENOUGH'.

Place the notes in places where you can see them, such as on the bathroom mirror, inside a wardrobe door that you open daily, on your laptop, etc.

Keep them visible everywhere so that your brain starts to believe the words and you begin to feel their meaning in everything you do.

Why is it so hard to be happy?

Do your unhappy periods outweigh your happy periods? If they do, have you ever wondered why that is?

One of the answers is that you may feel happy with what you have until you see someone else who appears to have more than you do, or something better.

You may feel happy with your wealth until you see someone with a bigger house or an expensive car; you may be happy with your work until you see someone else getting promoted, having more clients or getting recognised; you may be happy with your appearance until you see someone looking amazing; you may feel happy in your dynamic until you see someone getting engaged or married. We may be more disposed to feeling good when we aren't watching others; however, we can learn to also feel good when in company by working on our inner self and strength.

When we feel good within ourselves but our

contentment then dissolves the minute we see someone else's status, that is simply a reflection of our self-worth. This is because we have developed a deep belief system from childhood that causes us to think that we are in a state of constant competition and comparison with everyone else. We may be perfectly happy doing our own thing in our own time and space until we look around, at which point we create thoughts that say *They are doing it better* or *They are further ahead than me*. This leads to insecurity, fear, and stress.

Consider monks and nuns. They are at peace because their happiness stems from inside them. They have renounced their worldly possessions and attachments to material things; they no longer need 'things' to feel happy; they no longer find it necessary to compare their worth with someone else's. They have taken that control back; their progress and happiness depend only on themselves.

I was speaking to a nun, and she was telling me that at the place where they stay, they all have the same role; no one is above or below anyone else. They all wear the same clothes, so no comparisons can be made, and they are all addressed by first names only, so no caste or status is involved (this is still an issue is certain countries such as India). Their philosophy is about being equal to one another and united as one, with growth and inner peace as their only goals. I am not suggesting giving up anything but inviting you to start looking inwards rather than outwards.

I appreciate it is really hard not to compare oneself with other people especially with social media being present everywhere. We are now comparing ourselves not only with those we know but with all those we don't know, and we are allowing their lives to impact ours. We compare ourselves with celebrities, influencers and entrepreneurs.

We begin to add our own stories and emotions to the limited words they may have shared; we start to wish we had a life like theirs; we wish things were as easy as they appear to be for them; we wish we had their luxuries, their looks or their clothes; we wish people would validate and praise us as they do them; we end up wishing we *were* them. The more we wish we were someone else, the less we like ourselves; we start to focus on our flaws, and our stock of self-worth decreases. We look into the mirror and find flaws on our body; we look at our bank balance and think it's not enough; we look at our working life and believe we aren't doing enough; we look at our social life and think it's not sufficiently 'Instagrammable'.

If you were them, would you really feel happier? Some of you may feel that your happiness depends on others, but in reality, it depends on how you feel about yourself. You may say, 'Sheena, it's impossible not to compare myself with others and reflect on what I see.' It may be difficult not to see your imagined self in other people's lives, but what is controllable is how you respond to that.

Your happiness lies within you. IT ALWAYS HAS. I write this just after a day when Facebook, Instagram and WhatsApp went offline for a few hours meaning no one could access them. Wow! The number of posts I saw the day after when they were back online about how much people loved the social media-free time was incredible. People were forced to stop the scrolling and began to do other activities: playing with their children and pets for longer, doing some household chores and admin, calling friends, reading a book and so much more. People enjoyed using their time for something other than social media, and yet they only realised this when they were forced not to use it.

We very much conform to society and don't want to miss out, hence our slight addiction to social media. It's so important to take that control back. We can switch off social media and anything else that is no longer serving us usefully at any time we want to; those things don't have to control us. I have seen many people take a break from social media, and they felt incredibly uplifted by doing so.

If you know social media is a trigger for you, maybe you could start by reducing your time on it by ten minutes and then adjust it week by week until it's enough for you. Set yourself a timer when you go on it: for example, if you typically scroll for twenty minutes, time yourself so that you are only on it for ten.

Maybe you go on it when you are doing work or before bedtime or while you're watching TV. Again, maybe you can find ways to reduce your scrolling time, either by putting your phone in a different room or space or setting yourself a timer again for the length of time you want to be on it.

Start focusing on you and what makes YOU happy, not on what you think sounds or looks good to other people. If *YOU* want to be physically fitter and leaner, that's fine; if *YOU* want to purchase something for *YOU*, that's fine; if *YOU* are enjoying where you are at work, that's great; but if *YOU* want to progress for *YOU*, then that's also fine, as long as the reasons for your wants and desires are *YOURS* and not those of someone else.

You may perhaps have decided to stay in on a weekend, content being at home and having a relaxing day pottering around the house, resting in the garden and just being. Then, you happen to look on social media and you see people going to the beach or to restaurants or going out on day trips, and suddenly you don't feel so great. You start feeling like you've missed out on a better day and that you too should be out; being at home suddenly doesn't feel as good it did before you began looking at what other people were doing. Why does what felt good to you five minutes ago feel so meaningless now? Because you believe that other people wouldn't think what you were doing was 'fun' or 'interesting' or 'having a great time'. Their potential judgement and perception matter to you. You compared your good time with their image of a good time, and their image won the minute your mind started creating thoughts.

Your perception is what counts, so change it. Being at home having a free day just to be can feel like a luxury to some. I cherish days like this where I am not going anywhere, when I can potter from room to room, read a book, have some tea, go out in the garden, have a little nap, etc. A day full of those moments gives me total joy.

Days out are great, but days in are equally amazing, so don't underestimate the power of doing things in your time and in your way and doing what makes you feel good.

It's such an important topic because the lines can get blurred when you have to question whether what you want is really something for you or something that will make you look good to other people. Would we be thinking of things, wishing for them and doing them if we knew no one was going to watch? Would you do certain things if you knew you couldn't post them on social media for everyone to see and comment on?

I only started using social media about nine years ago. I only started using Instagram properly about eighteen months ago (at the time of writing this book). I remember in the early stages when I began using Facebook, about ten years ago at the time of writing this, I was at an extremely insecure and lonely stage in my life, with a consistent feeling of not being enough. I recall looking at people and their lives on Facebook, and this would highlight any voids I was feeling; if I saw people having a great time, it reminded me that I wasn't. If I saw people out with their friends, it reminded me that I didn't have many friends of my own. I remember putting posts and pictures up purely in the hope that someone would comment or make me feel valid and worthy. As social media grew (showing my age here) and phones became way smarter, it was very easy for people to click and upload, and so I too was caught in this circle of posting for feedback.

Now, at the time, I didn't have many friends. I struggled making friends as I grew up; I lost some friends along the way because of my anxiety and the impact it had on me, preventing me from doing things. University was the toughest period, as I struggled with my depression, and it was all I could do to just make it through and pass, and then when I married and moved to a new town, it was difficult to find new friends easily. What used to really impact me was when someone I knew posted something and received lots of comments and likes from their family and friends, whereas when I posted, I would never get the same response. I would always ask myself whether no one liked me, whether I was not enough. Again, I was letting my worth be defined by other people; the number of comments equalled my happiness: more comments meant more validation, and that meant a void was being filled, and that made me feel happier ... temporarily.

Over the years, I became aware that my happiness was becoming solely dependent on other people and was making me needy without my realising it. I also realised that I believed that external things would help me feel enough: a spa day, a dinner date, a holiday, etc., but this was a false assumption because the feeling of being enough was short-lived and temporary.

Let's return to the question posed by this chapter. Why is it so hard to be happy? It is only hard if you make it hard. Focus on yourself, your values, your wants, your joy; don't compare what you have with what others have. Their version of happiness won't be the same as yours. This doesn't mean they have more or less happiness than you; theirs is simply different. If you see someone on holiday while you are working, that doesn't mean they are happier than you; your happiness stems from within, not from a sought-after destination. If someone earns more money than you, that doesn't mean they are happier than you; happiness is not defined by wealth and objects. If you are looking for love and see someone getting married, it doesn't mean they are happier than you; happiness is not defined by another person. It is easy to think that all of these things and more equal a happier time, but unless you are happy exactly where you are right now, you will always be chasing happiness.

Happiness is truly practising acceptance until you align with it and believe in it. Happiness exactly where you are right now may sound nice, but you have to start believing it to feel it. Accept where you are right now; practise gratitude and be content for the present moment before you; focus on your journey forward, staying in your own lane at all times. Your future visions and dreams will only support your happiness if you are happy in this current moment.

Embrace your perfectly imperfect self

We are often made to conform at a young age especially if we go to certain mainstream schools. We are told to wear the same uniform, we are told to behave in certain ways, we are all taught the same things in the same way despite each and every one of us being completely unique in our dress sense, character and ways of learning. We try and fit in to make friends, we try not to draw too much attention to ourselves, we become self-conscious if we are too smart in case the other kids make fun of us or if we aren't academically smart and people again label us. We are labelled from an early age as the sporty kid, the shy kid, the loud kid, the smart kid or even the naughty kid.

We do what we can to be liked, to belong, to have friends and to persuade teachers to like us. Teachers may not always understand us, and with so many other children needing their attention, it can feel hard for us to learn in an environment where we all respond and progress differently. Some may like to learn quietly at their desks, others may like to be more expressive and creative, while some need extra support in certain areas; however, to be ourselves freely during the whole school day is impossible with so many rules and boundaries in place.

We may grow up in certain cultures, or our parents may have had certain standards and values that they imposed on us, such as the view that you have to have a good education to be successful, that you should follow a certain career path to be respected in society, that you need to earn a lot of money to be happy or that you must be married and have kids by a certain age. Despite the fact that we may not want to marry, may not want to have kids, may have dreams and plans of our own, we sometimes suppress these concerns in order to please our parents.

Our childhood conditions us to fit in because it's the safer option. We then become afraid to make changes or try and do different things. If we face challenges relating to our home life or the support and emotional attention we receive from our parents and carers, it can be hard to navigate our way through.

As an adult, it's important to remember you now have a voice and an opinion that you can use: you can choose whom you get to hang out with; you can choose what sort of hobbies and work to do; you can choose what to wear; you can choose where you want to go and where you don't. You can say yes to things, but you can also say no to things, and you can create healthy boundaries to ensure that you do what is right for you.

Embrace who you are; embrace it right now. Embrace your characteristics, your talent, your dress style, your body, the food you love, the places you love to visit and all your future dreams. Embrace it all. You don't have to conform to society, your friends or your family. You don't have to live by others' expectations of you; you are free and empowered to be who you want to be. Connect with the person you are beneath all the roles you play. Who are YOU when you aren't a son, daughter, sibling, parent, colleague, employee, owner, friend, etc.? Start connecting with the real you and getting to know that person.

You don't need to start making drastic choices if that feels too daunting and overwhelming; start with small changes. Discover who you are without reference to other people's opinions and influences. One of the small changes I started to make was simply saying no without the need to justify myself. An example is how I began to approach family trips: my parents and in-laws would come with us, and they loved to play cards in the evenings. I wasn't a huge fan of cards but always felt obliged to play to be sociable, even though I would have preferred curling up and reading a book instead. Over the years I just started saying no, or I would join in one game and then bow out for the next few. I would still be present, but while they played cards, I enjoyed my book. They did what they enjoyed, and I did what I enjoyed. It's been so important for me to emphasise this message to my children.

When I was a child, my parents, with the very best of intentions, would always tell me to join in with other kids or other activities, things that I really didn't want to do and felt uncomfortable with: they would tell me to 'go and join in with the disco', or 'go and talk to those kids over there', etc. I felt awkward and unhappy and felt that if I wasn't joining in, I wasn't good enough. I ensure my kids always have a choice. Would they like to go? Would they like me to come with them? Would they prefer to wait and join later? Are they happy just being? Sometimes our parents did it with the intention of 'boosting our confidence' or 'improving our social skills'; instead, it usually just made me feel that I wasn't good enough, especially compared with those who perhaps were joining in.

Be comfortable being you, and do what makes you feel good. Do what inspires you, and look for the right support when you need a little nudge or some encouragement. Start by saying no to the things that you don't feel like doing and yes to more of the things that inspire you.

The more you start being authentic and true to yourself, the more you will start living on your own terms. Start discovering who you are and what your identity is, and start living for you.

All aboard the train of life

People will come and go in your life as they do on a train journey. Many will board the train with you: some will already have been there from the start of the train's route, some will board later, some will stay on, others will get off; there is a moment of chaos when the doors open and people arrive and leave, but this doesn't impact your overall journey to your destination.

From the moment of your birth to where you are now, people will come and go in your life through various circumstances and situations. You may suddenly find that you are drifting apart from people you have known for years as you, or they, grow and change; there may be people you have tried to hang on to and devoted time and energy to, only to realise that they have never served any positive purpose in your life and still don't, and that it's time to let them go; you may know people who decide they no longer want you in their life; and you may experience a whole lot of new people arriving in your life at various stages.

Seeking human connections and needing to belong in a community with others are basic human survival instincts stemming from tribal times, where being with other people increased one's chance of survival. So, when changes to these connections occur in present times, it can initially be hard to cope with them and manage; we can feel a sense of panic, hurt and fear before we process our reactions and understand that changes sometimes occur for the best and for our higher good. Let's break this down.

Letting go of people who no longer give you joy

I am sure that many of you out there have family members or friends or colleagues that you have tried so hard to give your time and energy to and who never seem to reciprocate … and this has been going on for years. Especially when it comes to family members, you almost feel an obligation to give it your best shot: you want to form that bond and relationship with them, and you want to have a presence in their life and have them in yours. You want to feel good family vibes and share fun, love and laughter with them; you have images in your mind of great days spent together, meeting for coffee, going for dinner, hanging out at one another's homes, etc. You consistently make the effort and message them with suggested dates to do things, you check in on them every now and then, and you organise family get-togethers or days out, but you get little or nothing back from them.

You are always the first to contact them. If your paths cross, they never seem all that bothered about your presence; they make no real effort and don't go out of their way for you. You begin a vicious cycle of hoping things will change, questioning why they don't like you and wondering what's wrong with you and what you are doing wrong. Sometimes these feelings can intensify when you see your friends getting on well with other people.

Do you ever wonder whether their attitude towards you is something to do with them and their issues? How long will it be before you realise that maybe it's nothing to do with you at all? Just because they are linked to you biologically or through family, it doesn't give them the right to make you feel the way you do or to treat you with indifference. There is no pass for them just because they happen to be family or close friends.

Knowing you have given it your best and done everything with good intentions, you can allow them to get off the train at their destination and let go of the need to have them in your life. By letting go of them and of that need to connect and bond, you are creating space and energy for the people that truly do matter, making room on this train for your tribe to board it.

This isn't easy, and it's not about bluntly cutting ties and making that known to them; it's simply about preserving your own energy and no longer giving any of it to them. It's about not making the extra steps or effort any more, not sending those text messages and waiting in hope, not seeing them at events and hoping they include you; instead, it's about being civil and then doing your own thing.

Your mind will always wonder, and want to understand, why they couldn't give you what you needed; your heart will want those in question to understand the hurt they caused you, and you will want them to see and feel what you are going through and to care, and this will be the hardest emotion to surrender to but also the greatest thing you can do for yourself. Why? Because the truth is that you will never understand them or they you, because you are not them and they are not you.

Maybe you have let them know in the past of your feelings and nothing has been resolved, and maybe if you feel it's what you need to do, you can let them know your thoughts, but reflect before you make this choice. Do you really want this person or these people in your life? More years of feeling this way? If you choose to let them know your feelings and views, do it with no expectation of change. They may have been oblivious to how they were making you feel, or they may really not care; either way, let the outcome make no difference to how you move forward. Having an open conversation is a personal choice to make, and if you decide to go ahead, do it with the good intention of gently making them aware of your views without assuming a defensive or angry manner. Often, by simply letting go and focusing on your path, you can bring them to a deeper understanding of your feelings than you would by being confrontational. However you do it, simply let go. Let go for your peace and happiness.

The power lies in letting go of the need to understand and taking back the control of your emotions, which have been determined by others up until now. When you let the universe know that you are ready to surrender, ready to let go of these people, you are automatically creating space for new energies and people to come into your life.

When you grow apart from other people

As you grow, you may find you are changing as a person, in your thoughts, your interests and even your personality. Things that you may have liked previously may be different from those you like now; you may have enjoyed nights out before but now prefer to stay in; you may have lost interest in certain hobbies but gained an interest in new ones; your career path may be changing. And because of some of these changes, you may be noticing that you are drifting away from certain people in your life.

Some friends grow through the changes with you, while other friends may not fully understand the change in you; that's okay. You may have a history with some of these people, but there's no reason to ever force a friendship because that doesn't serve either of you. Some may not like the changes and will try to pull you back, keep on reminiscing about old times and continue to hold on to an older version of you; this is the time to be mindful that this isn't going to serve you in the long run. Stay true to who you are, and let them support your growth, or allow the relationship to fade. You don't need to cut it off completely, but you also don't need to feel guilty for not giving it so much time or energy if it's not healthy.

This can also happen the other way, and you may notice other people in your life changing. Again, you may still feel connected to a particular person, and the friendship will still continue, or you may feel that it's time to follow your own separate paths.

I'll shares a personal story with you. I had a childhood friend whom I had known since I was nine years old; we were good friends and had gone through a lot together. This friend shared with me some concerns regarding her husband, and I tried to support her and offer her guidance (we had helped each other like this for the past twenty years). The husband found out and wasn't happy at all, and he decided he didn't want her to be associated with me and basically advised her to end her friendship with me. We discussed this, and she said that every time we were in touch, it caused an argument between her and her husband, and she had decided it was best if we cut off our friendship. I was of course shocked and in tears; my friend was headstrong, and I would never have imagined her speaking or feeling like this or letting someone make her feel this way. However, there was nothing I could do, and since that phone call, we have never spoken again. People change, and sometimes you have to let it go and accept that change. I trust fully in the idea that some people are meant to enter your life only for a certain period of time, some will pop in and out of it and others will remain with you for a lifetime. But nothing is certain or guaranteed.

Those you surround yourself with really can uplift your energy or lower it, so choose your tribe carefully.

As you learn more about yourself over the years and as you become more comfortable in your own skin, you will have a clearer idea of whom you want in your life, and that won't be every single person you cross paths with. Don't spend time and energy trying to change others. It is not for you to change them; that is something only they can do should they wish to. The only changes you can make and control are those affecting you.

A lot of my closest friends have entered my life in the last few years because I have been true to myself and not tried to mould myself to fit in with someone else's life; those closest to me accept me for me and embrace all my perfect imperfections as I do with them. There are no longer the insecurities, waiting for that person to reply to text messages and wondering if they like me, or the need for them to make me feel valid. When you grow and embrace yourself, your friendships with others are much more genuine and stronger too.

New people and solitude

Be open to meeting new people and making new friends. You may cross paths with new people at various times in online forums, at clubs, in the gym, at work, etc. and find that you really enjoy their company. Even though it is human nature to stick to what we know, perhaps maintaining contact with long-term friends through habit when we no longer benefit from those relationships, it's important to connect with people who support us and give us joy.

We also don't need thousands of people to make us feel like we belong or even to make us feel happy; we technically only need ourselves. It is of course nice to have someone else to talk to and be social with, but just remember it's the quality of friendships that matters, not the quantity. I've worked with many clients who used to envy people who had a solid group of friends; one particular person would always find it difficult whenever she saw girl groups as she had never been part of such a group. She had always assumed that being part of a friendship circle where everyone went on holidays together, celebrated milestones together, became bridesmaids together, etc. would be incredible. This was based on her assumptions and the fact that she didn't feel whole or wanted from within, which was the main issue we worked on; the sense of belonging she saw in girl gangs was a trigger for her emotions. Learn to belong with yourself first; love yourself and feel whole just being you, then friendships will simply seem like a bonus and not a necessity.

It is also important to enjoy time alone. Being alone doesn't mean you are lonely. It means that you are comfortable when you are with others and when you are not, that you are happy in company and happy in solitude, that being with others doesn't automatically bring you happiness. Enjoy watching a movie on your own, reading a book, going for a walk and even taking yourself out for a coffee. I absolutely love having moments and time to myself, where I purposely have days in the diary that I don't plan to fill; this is my time, and time to myself is so precious. Always be mindful to have time to just be, to connect with yourself, to sit with your thoughts and do things you love … just with and for you.

So, as you continue on your path in life, accept that people will board the train and get off it at different times and that some will remain aboard until the final station. Your destination won't change, but your journey will become more enriched. Everyone has a purpose for coming on board whether they stay or leave; take a moment to see what the ones who leave have taught you. Maybe they have shown you the values that you align with; maybe they have taught you that change is inevitable; maybe they have enabled you to recognise your own growth; and maybe they have shown you that the only person you truly need to depend on is *YOU*.

Being open and honest with yourself and others

It is so important to stay open and honest with yourself about how you feel and who you are at all times. Doing things that make you uncomfortable, doing things because of pressure, doing things to fit in and belong: these behaviours will never be of value to you in the long run. I learnt this the hard way.

In the midst of my anxiety, I had major issues like not being able to eat in front of other people (or limiting myself in what I did eat); I used to always be conscious if I dropped or spilt something or if there was food in my mouth, and I had real fear of judgement and embarrassment. I also had a fear of driving to new places: I would be afraid of getting lost and not being able to park, especially if there were other people watching me. These and other issues led to huge social anxiety and a dislike of going to places if I didn't know the people there very well or if I knew that those attending were super confident and outgoing.

I would consistently make up excuses not to go to certain events or gatherings even if they were just in people's homes, or if I did go, I would say I had a headache so that I could leave early. This led to some people believing I wasn't making enough effort, that I wasn't trying to be sociable, that I wasn't doing what others expected of me in the context of our relationships. I didn't blame them, because they had zero awareness of my anxieties and I had zero idea that I was suffering with anxiety, believing that this was just who I was born to be. In their eyes, though, I simply could have done better.

I continued to be known as the unsociable one, the quiet one, the shy one, etc., and this went on for many years. I did everything I could to avoid social situations or reduce my time in them.

As the years passed and I began to understand and get support for my anxiety, I learnt to embrace my perfectly imperfect self. I realised that it was okay to be who I was and be honest about it; it was okay to try and work through the issues and let people know that's what I was doing.

I began telling people that I found it hard in social settings, and so my friends would take steps to support me, such as walking into gatherings together with me or ensuring they were looking for me when I arrived. It was this extra bridge of support that I needed to be able to help myself in making progress. It also felt like a huge relief to just be open and honest about who I was; there was no more making excuses or people assuming things about me that were simply untrue. I felt so much freer, and what I found was the people that supported me were my genuine friends, the ones that wanted me to progress and move forward.

It's also important to be honest in what you want to do. There may be times when your friends want to go out when you fancy a night in, or they may have arranged or suggested an activity that really doesn't interest you or has come at a time when you are really busy. It's okay to be honest and say no; it's okay to be honest about the reason why; and it's okay to stay true and not always conform with what others are doing.

I've been part of gym groups where the majority have taken part in activities like Tough Mudder, while I have had zero interest in joining in … and that's okay. I have had people invite me to activities where I want to give it a go but have felt nervous, as they were new me, and so I've simply said that. It's nice to just be open and be free with the thoughts and feelings knowing that everyone else may be feeling something similar and that they may be able to support you.

It's also really important to know and remember that you are never alone in your thoughts; it's likely that others are also feeling some of what you are feeling or that they have experienced similar feelings before. Often, we think it must just be us who have certain thoughts and feelings and concerns about situations, but the truth is that many other people share our worries. I am sure many of you will have seen posts on social media groups that make you laugh but also make you say: 'Wow! I honestly thought it was just me that thought that.'

Most people will feel a little anxious walking into a social event alone; most people (no matter how long they have been doing it) will feel nervous when delivering a presentation; most will be apprehensive when they have to start something new or go somewhere or do something that is unfamiliar. There will be a million thoughts crossing people's minds all the time. Some will have small worries, while others will have larger ones; most of us don't share our thoughts, and therefore we assume everyone has it together and is winning at life … when really, we are all just winging it. Remember that the thought of something is usually worse than the reality; our mind has a great imagination and loves to escalate thoughts, so always learn to train it and keep it in check. It's like a puppy that has you running all over the place and leaves you feeling exhausted; however, once trained, the dog listens to your commands, and it respects and loves you. The mind is exactly the same. You have to learn to control it and not allow it to control you.

I remember going to a training meeting recently. We were discussing our daily lives at work, and as soon as one person was open about their worries (she said she often woke up at 3 a.m. wondering if she had done the right thing for her patients), others opened up about their similar thoughts, with a surge of relief as they shared their feelings. Up to that point, we had all appeared to have everything under control and be as cool as cucumbers.

If you look hard enough, you will always find people to support your journey and your growth, but at all times, be your own biggest support and cheerleader because no one can cheer you on like you can.

Perception

There are two definitions of PERCEPTION:

1. The ability to see, hear or become aware of something through our senses;
2. The way in which something is regarded, understood or interpreted.

Perception can truly make a difference to so many of our experiences and interactions. One of the main reasons we feel aggrieved or unable to let go of hurt caused, or perceived to be caused, by other people is how we interpret things. Our interpretation will be based on our past experiences and how we have been made to feel previously. Our brain subsequently uses our stored emotions to colour its version of the context of words and actions.

For example, imagine there is someone in your life whom you don't particularly like, as they've not always been the kindest or nicest of people in their dealings with you. However, they may be trying to change, to make more effort or to be nicer, but because of your past experiences, you now view everything they say or do with a critical eye. You interpret their text message as being blunt, short, or without feeling when in reality they were perhaps nervous about sending you a message or too busy to write a long one; perhaps that's just how they write texts to everyone. When you meet up with them, you will always look for their flaws or for things they could have done better. You may entertain critical thoughts: *She didn't say hello straight away, She didn't ask about my children, She could have made more effort in her choice of gift*, etc. An unbiased person witnessing the same situation may have perceived it as being thoughtful that she offered a gift at all, that she came over specifically to say hello and acknowledge you, that she asked about other things before being called away.

Remember that just because you think something, that doesn't make it a reality. Your perception of the friend who is successful and rich and seems to have it easy is exactly that … a perception. So, when that friend doesn't always check in or often says she's busy, your perception causes you to think: *Busy doing what? You have it so easy. Surely if I can find the time to message you, then you can message me too*. It is important to appreciate that we really don't know it all; we need to practise being open-minded and non-judgemental.

When people don't follow society's rules – the passenger on the bus who doesn't give up a seat for an elderly person, the person who is rude or abrupt, the parents who don't speak with their children when they're misbehaving – we make assumptions about those people. We perceive them to be unkind or not in control when in reality, there could be valid reasons for every type of behaviour and action.

I used to take everything so personally, and if I

crossed paths with someone I wasn't a huge fan of or received a text message from them, I would always get my husband to give me his view because it would very likely be different from mine. My perception would be based on my feelings and past emotions in regard to this person, and I would twist it to fit in with my preconceived position. I would read the text out in a certain tone or with particular mannerisms when in reality it was a simple and emotionally neutral message.

Even a simple message such as 'have a great day' can be perceived in various ways depending on how you feel towards someone. For example, your reaction might be: 'How lovely! They are wishing me a nice day,' or 'Couldn't they have written more than that?' or 'Are they really wishing me a great day or secretly hoping I have bad one?' or 'That doesn't seem genuine,' when in reality, their message may be no more than a general greeting with no ulterior motive.

Minds are like parachutes – they work best when open
(Thomas Dewer)

Fear of what others think

These are five words that have one of the biggest impacts on us, our decisions, our actions and ultimately our life path. We often worry about what others think before considering what we ourselves think; that's fine if you do that because you think it may impact those people, but not if you simply fear their opinion. We fear their opinion because we fear rejection, which speaks to our tribal survival instinct and our innate need to belong.

How much are you missing out on by not giving things a go because you worry what others may think? How much opportunity and experience are you depriving yourself of?

How many times have you walked past a clothes shop and fancied trying on what was on the mannequin in the window but never have because it might not suit you or it's not your usual style or others might laugh if you adopt a new style?

Have you ever seen a new class at the gym, or heard that one of your friends was trying a new club or hobby that sounded fun or interesting and thought *I'd love to give that a go* but feared not knowing what to do, not being good enough, or getting things wrong and becoming the object of other people's judgement?

Have you ever wanted to go for a promotion, try a new challenge in your line of work or even start up a new business? The thought of what others may think, whether in your workplace or even among friends and family, has stopped your thoughts turning to action.

Have your friends ever wanted to you to dance with them or your children wanted you to go on some playground apparatus or take part in sports day but you've been held back by fear?

We worry about standing out, about being different, about hearing words from others or seeing looks on their faces that may make us feel uncomfortable, embarrassed and unsure about ourselves. Now, I absolutely know this is a normal human response, and we will most likely always wonder what others think, but there are two things that will make a difference to your mindset:

1. Wondering about people's opinions;
2. Fearing people's opinions.

So, what do I mean by this? When you are wondering what someone may say when you do something different, you are simply curious about their thoughts. You wonder what their response may be and what feedback they will give you, but whatever it is, you are okay either way, and it won't impact on your action. They may seem surprised at your choices, give you some criticism that's not entirely constructive, not give you the support you would have liked or not show any enthusiasm, and they may question your ability, but that doesn't stop you going ahead with your actions. You are confident of giving things a try regardless.

When you fear someone's opinions, that fear is strong enough to stop you moving forward. You take their opinion personally and to heart; their opinion, in your mind, is like a fact. If someone made you doubt your ability at the new gym class, or if someone said that your dream of a new career was crazy or that a certain style didn't suit your appearance or that your new partner wasn't right for you, you would believe them and act accordingly, because you lack self-belief and self-worth.

Thoughts such as *What if they said this? What if they thought that? What if they laugh at this?* etc. ultimately lead to this question: 'What if they think I am not good enough?' You fear someone confirming the story that you have created and made strong in your mind that you are not enough. This fear stems from past experiences that haven't been processed or upgraded. The fear of failure or rejection, of things possibly not going to plan, outweighs the possibility of things working out exactly as you hoped or of you at least being confident in trying to see where an idea leads you.

There have been times when I have wanted to try new business ideas, unique outfits and accessories, or new ideas in my workplace, or when I have been interested in exploring new classes at my local gym. Fear has entered my mind, and I have worried about the consequences if a plan didn't work out or if other people judged me, but ultimately, I have worked on reminding myself that I am doing things for me and not for anyone else. What's the worst that could happen? I was told numerous times by various people that it wasn't worth the time, effort and money to start a new business and that I should stick with my current job, which did make me hesitate and wonder whether I should pursue my goal. But I did start a new business, and yes, it has been hard, but it has also been incredible, rewarding and a beautiful experience. Your dreams and hopes are yours to experience so that you can say, 'I did that, I gave it a go, I succeeded, and I learnt something,' and ultimately have no regrets later on in life. It is of course harder when the support you require from those close to you isn't there, but as you work on yourself, you will realise the greatest support you have is within you.

I wore a weird and wonderful hat on a trip to London once, and random strangers actually stopped me to say they loved my hat – it was a snowman hat with little woolly arms sticking out of it. It wasn't sophisticated, glam or chic, but it was fun and cute, and I loved it … so I wore it for *ME*.

I've gone to the gym and been a beginner in a class: my legs and arms didn't coordinate, I lifted my left leg when the whole class were lifting their right one, I could only fold over and reach my thighs when the whole class were reaching their toes, I didn't change gears on the spin bike when the instructor was advising us to, because

I was just too knackered ... but I got through the class. There were people who were incredibly flexible, people who were spinning as if their life depended on it, people who had all the energy and stamina in the world ... or more than me anyway.

Rather than feeling not good enough, I changed my story and reminded myself that I was there, being courageous in showing up, being brave in giving it a go, doing the best I could that day, which was an improvement on what I had done yesterday. It was progression, not perfection, and that was enough for me: let that be a reminder that it should be enough for you too.

You may fear taking part in your child's sports day or you may worry about wearing a bikini on your holiday or going on a team activity with friends or colleagues where you are nervous of not being good at the activity simply because you are concerned about what others may think.

I'll say it over and over again, and I want you to repeat it over and over again ... people's judgements are a reflection on them and not on you. Live for you, have fun for you, learn and grow for you, experiment for you, change your mind a thousand times if you want to, and do what feels right for you. There's no shame or embarrassment in pivoting and changing as many times as you need to. There's no shame in saying, 'I gave it a go but decided it wasn't for me.' It's okay not to be great at something as long you have fun; it's okay to fall over and mess up just as it is to be great and win. Enjoy the moments, all the perfectly imperfect moments. It's also important to remember that people care less than you think. I repeat: *PEOPLE CARE LESS THAN YOU THINK,* in the nicest possible way. People are usually too focused on their own actions and thoughts to worry about how your bikini looks or how you are running in the sports event.

I set up a plant-based food business. I was asked many times why I was doing it and why I was adding extra pressure to my life. I was an optometrist and also running a well-being business; now I was starting a food business, initially without a clue as to where to start. However, I wanted to do it, I wanted to explore it, and it took me on an amazing journey. I supplied cool shops and restaurants, I met new people, I ran food stalls. One of my favourite memories was taking my kids with me to a food fayre when I had no childcare. They loved it so much. I even won an award for my brownies. However, after five years, I decided it was no longer for me. I had other dreams to pursue and couldn't balance everything.

It's okay to start or stop something; it's okay to begin and then decide you don't actually like it; it's okay to start and find it harder than you thought. It really is ALL okay because you will find your way; the hardest thing is not starting at all and wondering 'what if …?'

- What thoughts have crossed your mind whilst reading this?
- What things do you want to try?
- What's one step you can take to get closer to making it happen?
- What can you do to commit to taking this step?
- When can you do this?

What fears are holding you back? Write them down, and remind yourself that magic happens outside of your comfort zone. Read them, then cross them out and instead write down this: 'Despite this thought, I am going to do it anyway.'

Remind yourself of the following: you owe it to yourself to try your best and to live your hopes and dreams, and the only one that can make it happen is you. Tell yourself this: 'I am okay with whatever the outcome may be as long as I know I gave it a go. I am excited to see the future unfold.'

Relationships with a partner

You are not responsible for each other's happiness

I have talked a lot about relationships with friends, family and colleagues, but I want to go a little deeper and talk about relationships with your partner and whether the relationship you have right now is healthy or toxic.

When we think of a relationship between two people, we envision those two people caring for each other, loving each other, supporting each other and growing together through life's journey. It sounds simple enough, but in reality, this takes a lot of work, communication and effort on both sides.

These two people may have a connection and be attracted to each other for a variety of reasons; however, they are still individuals with their own dreams, beliefs, needs and past experiences.

There are many things to consider when going into a relationship and during the relationship.

Dependant or saviour?

Your role can never be to save someone, and you cannot expect your partner to save you. When your partner has their own struggles, including depression, anxiety, childhood trauma, childhood abuse, unhealthy addictions, anger issues and more all stemming from past issues and wounds, it is not your role to fix them. Supporting them and being responsible for their healing and happiness are very different things, and it is so important to have that boundary clear and in place both in your minds and in your communication.

Supporting them and encouraging them to take the right steps forward through professional support, talking to others, looking at support groups, etc. is being there for them and suggesting ways they can obtain help.

Taking on their struggles and issues, albeit with good intentions, will never work in the long run. Talking to them constantly, finding ways to cheer them up and putting up with the emotional roller coaster of them being great on some days and low on others can all put a huge emotional strain on you. You are almost living for that person and not for yourself, putting your own goals, social life and needs on hold, being there for them and not yourself in the hope that one day things will change.

You may not even realise how much of an impact it's having on you until much later on. Your nights out with friends become fewer because they stop asking you to join them; your progression at work slows as you struggle to function and stay motivated; your own energy decreases as you try and hold both of you up.

You take their love and their belief in you as a message that you have to do this for them; you can't let them down in their hour (that becomes months) of need. You feel guilty if the thought of doing so crosses your mind because they have no one else and you are the only one they trust and confide in.

Nobody can fix that person apart from that person. As hard as this may be for them, the responsibility to make a change for themselves lies within them, and this dependency on another person is unhealthy for both of you. If they want you to be happy and the relationship to work, then they need to take that control and responsibility and put in the work for themselves. Of course, you can be there during this time, but you are not their sole source of support.

If this sounds familiar to you, then your first step is right there: acknowledging the situation. The next step is communicating this to your partner, and this will be the toughest one because emotions will rise from hurt where your partner thinks you don't care, to anger or fear, as your partner may begin to panic and experience negative thoughts that include the feeling that they are being abandoned. This step will be hard, but it's important to stay focused as you separate facts from fiction. You do care, and knowing that is what you need to hold on to as you both navigate through this time.

Trust that working on this will make your relationship much healthier and help you on your way to a future that can really be bright for both of you.

Speaking from my own experience, when I was struggling profoundly with my own mental health, I was heavily reliant on my husband. I needed him for everything: to listen to me for hour after hour; to hold me as I cried endlessly; to sit outside my locked room and talk me out of my escalating wild thoughts; to cancel plans or leave events early, as I couldn't face people. He never complained or said a word, and I had no idea at the time how mentally drained he must have been, how he was trying his absolute best with zero support from anyone because no one knew the situation and how exhausting all that must have been. Our relationship was wonderful when I was okay; it was not so wonderful when I wasn't. He never once complained or made me feel it wasn't wonderful, but looking back, I realise just how much he was carrying me and how tough that would have been for him.

It was only when I made a conscious decision to do more to support myself, to find professional support, to read motivational books and to do the inner work for myself that the changes occurred.

I grew as a person. I was no longer being carried; I felt more alive and independent and, more than anything, an equal in the relationship. I had spent a long time feeling useless, incapable and not good enough, including as a wife, and always feeling he deserved better, but after taking that responsibility and working on myself, I felt whole again, excited and ready for the future ahead. It takes time and patience, but healing your inner self can bring about the most wonderful changes and the most incredible opportunities in your life as you see things through a new lens.

If you are the one in the relationship who is going through emotional issues, this is a reminder that you cannot rely on your partner to save you or believe that they are responsible for your happiness and healing.

Just because they know your story, your journey and your highs and lows, you cannot see or use them as your comfort blanket forever. You cannot rely on them to be your pick-me-up every time you hit a low, to save you every time you crash. It may be the easy thing to do, but it's not healthy, and in the long term, it will cause more damage to you and your relationship than good.

Dig deep, and write down an action plan to get you moving forward for yourself, including seeing your GP, seeing a therapist, calling a support line, looking for online or in-person support groups, etc. Speak to family, friends or colleagues, and get additional support. Find a motivational book or podcast to help you through the journey. Make a daily action plan and work on yourself every day, making your biggest motivator the act of asking yourself WHY? with your answer being that you want to achieve happiness, peace and independence for yourself and in your relationship.

Neither one of you can support the other fully without healing yourselves first. You can't serve someone if your own cup is empty or has a hole in it. There may be fear that if you start doing things for yourself, your partner will stop caring as much. This is a normal thought to have, but it is definitely not what will happen. Being a happier, healthier version of you means you will have an even stronger relationship together.

Toxic relationships

A toxic relationship can be defined as one where there is conflict, competition, disrespect, emotional and physical abuse, and a consistent lack of trust.

These behaviours, which may or may not be intentional, are highly likely to have stemmed from past experiences. The individual may have had a difficult upbringing as a child, seen their parents in a toxic relationship with each other, been bullied in their school years, had other troubled relationships or experienced other forms of trauma.

In a relationship where physical abuse is present, intervention needs to happen immediately, and both individuals should separate and seek professional support before deciding on how to move forward.

Take a moment to think if your relationship:

- Makes you feel sad;
- Makes you feel lonely;
- Damages your self-esteem and self-worth;
- Causes you anxiety;
- Causes you anger or frustration;
- No longer brings joy or excitement;
- Causes you to feel uncomfortable around your partner;
- Makes you feel like you are walking on eggshells.

Individuals can make you feel as if you are to blame; they may make you feel guilty and may subtly or blatantly end up controlling you and your role in the relationship. Sometimes, the signs and red flags are hard to see, especially if you are not aware of them and therefore not looking for them, and you may have been together for so long that the situation appears almost normal to you.

Instead of having supportive conversations with you filled with care and kindness, the partner is more likely to use sarcasm, make rude and flippant comments or offer only criticism and accusations. You avoid each other, or they are controlling, constantly wanting details about your movements and actions.

Your own self-care becomes non-existent, you stop looking after your needs, you don't go out, and you don't make time for hobbies; instead, you become withdrawn, struggling to find joy in anything.

This is not to say that things can't work out, but BOTH sides have to put the effort in, both sides have to commit to making and creating changes, both sides have to work on themselves, and both sides have got to want to do all this.

Showing awareness, accepting responsibility for the role you've played, working on past issues and wounds, exploring external support, and ensuring regular communication are all foundational behaviours in the creation of a better relationship and future.

It's often very easy to shift the blame, saying 'if he wasn't like that' or 'if she didn't behave like that' or 'if they didn't say that', etc., and falsely believe you are not accountable at all. However, being understanding and open and less defensive can ease the aggression on both sides; when you accept some of the responsibility, the other person may do so too. If you are the one being accused and you know your partner is not willing to change, then maybe it is time to step away.

Repairing a relationship will take time and patience. There will be hurdles and setbacks, but during the blips, it's important to remember not to bring up the past or use it in quick insults; avoid saying things in the heat of the moment that you may later regret.

Talk and communicate with each other about your thoughts and feelings. Avoid accusations, and talk instead about how certain actions make you feel. Listen, so that the other person feels heard, and ensure you are feeling heard too. Very often, we are simply thinking of what we want to say back during a conversation rather than listening 100 per cent.

Give each other time, understanding and care, and consider each other with compassion as you work through this together. Therapy or professional support can also really help on this journey.

Healthy relationships

A healthy relationship is one in which you work on yourselves every day as well as working together towards your shared future.

A healthy relationship between two individuals involves giving each other time and space to grow and develop but also giving your support to each other's goals and dreams. You want the other person to succeed, thrive and be happy.

Being happy and content within yourself allows you to be genuinely happy for the other person. There is no competition, no ego, no dependency; instead, there is healthy mutual respect and a commitment to do better for yourself and for each other.

Maintaining a healthy relationship is not easy, and there will be bumps along the way because you won't always know the right thing to say or do; it will be a process of growth with a significant learning curve, but that's okay because it's a journey you are on together.

Remember that your partner isn't your 'better half' or your 'other half'; you are COMPLETE just being you.

Having somebody in your life is about sharing moments and experiences together and individually; it's about supporting each other's dreams and your own too; it's about being happy about your partner's progress and journey whilst working on your own happiness too; it's about agreeing to disagree at times and having different opinions; it's about listening, respecting and being heard too. It's about compromising, communicating and being open-minded.

Can you be happy for someone else without feeling sad for yourself?

This is a really hard question and one where you will have to be very honest with yourself. When you hear good news from other people – a friend who's gone on a wonderful vacation, bought a gorgeous new house or found a new relationship; a colleague who has been offered a dream job; perhaps a family member sharing wedding or baby news – you hear yourself congratulate them and you are genuinely happy for them and want the best for them, but deep inside you feel the absence of the things you are lacking even more.

It's hard when you want to feel their joy and celebrate their success and yet their news makes you stop and reflect; you feel a sense of sadness come over you. It makes you think of the relationship you desire but don't have yet; you think of your own work progression and maybe not yet getting to where you need to be; you evaluate your own social life – or your lack of one.

You start adding emotions and stories to your ruminations, the thoughts begin to spiral, and you begin to come to the conclusion that your life isn't so great after all, that you aren't doing enough, that you haven't achieved enough. You don't feel as 'lucky' as others, and you sense a void opening up.

It's a natural human reaction to feel this way. The feeling can last from minutes to hours to days; it can be mild, or it can be deep if there are additional triggers. Your feelings are normal and they are valid; it's what you do with them that matters.

Use this reflection productively instead of being consumed by sadness or staying in a wishful state. Use it as a time to think about what it is you do want from life, and write down some goals and plans to work towards. If your aim is a relationship, you will want to consider the safe ways in which you can meet new people; if it is a new house, then think about ways you can save money, and look at your current financial position and the type of house you would like; if it is a vacation, then pick up a brochure or look online at what is available that suits you. Sounds simple? That's because it is: when you focus your energy on your journey, that's when you will see change. I'm not saying these things will happen overnight, but you can make a start in moving towards your goals. Spend more time on them and less on other people's lives.

Someone else's happiness doesn't mean you don't get to be happy, someone else's joy doesn't mean you don't get to experience joy, and someone else's good news doesn't mean you won't get good news. You don't get to see the other person's whole story or journey. Very few people receive anything overnight or easily, and the chances are that if what someone has was somehow gained through luck, it will be hard work for them to keep hold of it. So, when you see yourself looking at someone's life and a twinge of envy pops in, acknowledge it, then wish that person the best, and focus your energy back on you.

When you begin to feel true joy and happiness for others, you let go of any resistance within you. Resistance is an energy that blocks your own abundance from becoming available to you. As you feel joy for others and let go of any outcomes you desire for yourself, you start to attract the energy of flow. When you really want something, when you really feel like you need it, you are creating a force that is running against the current; this force of desire will prevent you from having what you crave because the universe wants you to see that you do not need it in order to be happy. So, my point here is this: work for it, give it your time and energy, but don't expect it to happen instantly or without some rerouting along the way. Surrender to the outcome. For example, when you have submitted a job application or emailed someone and are waiting for a response, checking your email or your phone for missed calls won't speed up the process, so use that time to take some other productive step.

This is also a good place to remember that even if you have it ALL, it still won't mean you feel joy or happiness permanently, because happiness comes from within. Until you are content just being as you are right now, you will forever be searching for things to make you happy. So absolutely work on your goals and dreams, but work on your inner self too.

The version of you that is wherever you are right now reading this book is already enough without needing any more, so get to know that person better. Without the extra accessories of life, you are still enough; your simplest form is the form that is most clearly enough. Know that everyone's extras in life come with added pressures and responsibilities; it's not all happy smiles and feel-good moments. Loving exactly where you are at right now is the greatest foundation to build upon; thereafter, the extras will be exactly that – extras that can create intermittent feel-good moments. But the constant feel-good moment will come from within you.

Every single thing that would seemingly be incredible if you had it comes with work, commitment and dedication. Getting married is a beautiful commitment, but it will require daily input from both individuals to make it successful. Having children can be a wonderful gift, but that of course comes with many unknowns and rewarding yet challenging phases. I've known people land dream jobs and homes that they have loved, but everything like that comes with problems that you have to navigate through.

Keep working on your inner world so that you can respond to the outer world as it waits to deliver you your dreams.

Life will test you until you learn the lesson it's trying to teach you: life triggers

Do you ever find yourself repeatedly in the same scenario or situation? Do the same people or type of people trigger your emotions and beliefs over and over again?

Another failed job interview? An ex that you keep seeing on social media? A family member you see often who never makes you feel good? A 'friend' who keeps making hurtful comments? Things that you felt you had moved on from, forgotten or got over keep triggering the same emotions; the hurt comes flooding back, the reactions remain the same, and you feel like you are back at square one.

Life has a way of showing you the same or similar scenarios until you have learnt to manage your mindset and your response to situations; only then will you be able to move on to the next layer of life.

Only very recently, I was involved in a situation with

a friend, which was triggering some old wounds, and I knew that life was presenting me with this situation as a test. I had done the mindset work and some of the inner work, and it was almost as if I was being given a practical test to put into practice what I had learnt. Was I going to break the emotional cycle and respond differently? Was I going to be able to let it go and not have it consume me? The test felt so clear, and even though the emotions were rising, I knew this was a moment in which I had to change the way I saw things. I let go of my expectations, of what I thought was right and wrong, and I surrendered to what was. I didn't need that certain outcome to make me happy; I looked at everything else that I was so grateful for instead. I continued to reframe my thoughts and challenge my mindset anytime I felt as if I was going backwards, reminding myself to create new thoughts and beliefs and strengthen and rewire my neural pathways.

In the weeks that followed, some wonderful and unexpected news and people entered my life. I knew then that the universe had given me a valuable lesson and that I had learnt so much from it, but I was also aware that the lesson had been given to me many times over the last fifteen years ... Yes, that's how long it had taken me to learn.

THERE IS A DIFFERENCE BETWEEN GIVING UP AND LETTING GO.

You are not giving up on the situation or person but rather letting go of what isn't serving you and instead receiving peace and freedom in your inner self.

Let's take the failed job interview scenario. You may think you will never catch a break, that you simply aren't good enough, that others are always better than you, etc., and you may well be floating in this sea of thoughts. Let's change the narrative: this wasn't the right position for you; what can you learn from it so that, when the right position does come, you can be even better prepared? Think about all the wonderful things you already have; let go of the belief that that particular role would have made you happier. When you are genuinely at peace with where you already are, the next opportunity will always present itself at a time when you are not expecting it.

I hope you become more mindful and aware that if you are facing the same situation over and over in life, the next time you face it, you can respond to it differently. Take a moment to think about the similar situations that keep cropping up for you, how you have felt each time they occurred, and how or if they got resolved. You may say that the other person in that situation was responsible for causing your hurt and pain; because of their actions and words, you felt upset. Yes, maybe that person's actions and words did cause hurt, maybe they were entirely in the wrong and you were completely right, maybe the situation was really heartbreaking and demotivating. However, you can't control or change that or them. You can sit in the pool of hurt or you can do something about it. It always comes down to you, not to the situation or the people involved in it.

Other people cannot control your emotions unless you let them. You can wish and hope for better friends, siblings, colleagues, parents, in-laws, etc.; you can continue to question why they behave the way they do; you can continue to wonder why they can't be nice; but you will never fully know the answers, and all the wondering will simply eat away at your time and energy. You can feel like a failure or feel not good enough following the failed job interview or other setback, but what purpose does that serve? There is always a choice in how you move forward, and again, it took me years to get out of my cycle of thoughts. I was constantly yo-yoing between self-pity, thinking I was destined for a life of not being good enough, and wanting others to know the hurt they had caused me, wanting answers to the never-ending questions that circled in my mind. I had given up control, and for years, my thoughts dragged me from one place to another, and I got nowhere; I remained in the same state and place of anxiety and unhappiness.

Emotional triggers will be exactly that unless you keep breaking them. Ever had a time when you felt you had moved on and got over a person or situation, and then bam! out of nowhere, something happens and you are triggered again? These triggers will keep coming unless you really face the cause of them. What do you need to do to let go of this wound? What do you need so that you can heal from this that doesn't require any action from the people who trigger you?

If you have done your absolute best, if you have worked as hard as you can, if you have given your best efforts with the best of intentions, then that is sufficient; you have done more than enough. The people causing your hurt are not worth it. Why waste any more time and energy on them? Let go of the notion that they need to understand you and you need to understand them. You don't have to get on with everyone you cross paths with. You won't be everyone's cup of tea, and everyone won't be yours – and that's okay.

With any setbacks, you should aim to learn, grow and develop. Does that sound harsh? It's not meant to be. What is the other option? Yes, there will perhaps be deeper-rooted issues affecting why you aren't feeling as though you are enough, and these experiences will trigger them, but taking small steps to change your mindset and thought process will slowly start breaking this cycle.

I have had endless rejections, and things have not gone my way at certain times. I used to take it all personally, thinking it must just be me because all those other people out there appear to be thriving. The truth was that it wasn't my time; I had to keep growing and learning – and that was okay, the key was not to give up. Let the rejections and setbacks come. Embrace them, but keep trying and keep going.

IT'S NOT EASY. The journey is hard, but the rewards are really worth it. So, when you experience a setback, take some time to process what you are feeling, separate the facts from the fiction, and write down what you are feeling. It's absolutely not about brushing problems under the carpet; it is very important to acknowledge your feelings, but then doing something to manage them is equally important.

Do something that makes you feel good for a short period: going for a run, watching a movie, listening to music, reading a book, calling a friend. Allow your tension to ease, and then take a moment to write down your thoughts and feelings again. Do they seem less intense or a little clearer?

Now make a list of all the things that show just how far you've come: all your skills, knowledge, traits and qualities that make you who you are today. You probably feel that you can't do this, right? That you can't think of anything worthwhile. Or that it simply feels weird writing things about yourself. It may feel uncomfortable, but this is an important practice in building yourself up, and hopefully a practice that makes the uncomfortable soon feel comfortable.

Let me start you off … You learnt to walk after falling multiple times, right? You learnt to feed yourself. You maybe have some qualifications. You've shown kindness to someone. You helped somebody out. You've learnt some skills. You've learnt to be independent. You're considerate and caring. You try hard in all you do. You are a good friend. Keep adding things to this list that are relevant to you, no matter how small or basic you think they seem.

You really are stronger, braver, wiser, more valid and more worthy than you give yourself credit for. Give yourself a hug or a high five or both, and let's step it up to plan moving forward.

If a life situation has set you back or disappointed you, let's reset and go again. What have you learnt? What feedback, if any, was given? What could you do differently next time? What can you research? Who can you ask for support from? Be practical: make a list of all the steps you can take going forward, and let's try again. Let go of the ifs and buts; there will be more opportunities coming for you, so let's do everything we can to get ready for them.

If the same people repeatedly hurt you, then maybe now is the time to consider stepping away from them. If this pattern has been repeating itself, the chances are that things won't change and you will continue to find yourself in a hurtful position, so let them go; you don't need to try any more, and you don't need to understand their actions. Distance yourself from them; don't try and get in touch with them hoping for a better response or for them to change; avoid places where your paths may cross; if you do happen to encounter them, don't feel any obligation to make an effort. Let these people fade away from your life.

You may say, 'But Sheena, some of these people are my family members. I can't just let them fade out of my life.' I understand you may think that, but actually you can let them go; it doesn't have to be an abrupt or obvious ending or separation. Sometimes, even those who are closest to us biologically can be the ones who impact us the most. Just because they are related biologically, they don't the right to hurt you, and you don't have to spend a lifetime trying to prove yourself or making them understand you. You also don't need to spend your life trying to make them like you. You can't change ANYONE, including family. And yes, this will be hard to accept, but it's something you will have to do to move on.

Acknowledge your feelings, but practise letting go of what isn't serving you; the longer you hold on, the more energy will be drained from you and the harder it will be to move on. I'm sure you can remember incidents from a year ago, five years ago, even ten years ago that caused you pain. You will remember the setting, the words that were spoken, what you were wearing, etc. because that hurtful moment is so embedded in your mind. You've been carrying that hurt for so long, in the hope of what? That someone will come and apologise? That someone will beg for forgiveness or realise their errors? Or do you keep replaying the conversations that with hindsight you could have had? You have to preserve your energy. Your mind is your responsibility, as are your peace and happiness, so let go of that event. And let go of that person: wish them well and focus back on your path.

Doing nothing is doing something

Technically, even if you are simply resting, sitting still, sleeping or staring out of the window, you are still doing something. However, what I really mean for the purposes of this chapter is that one person's version of doing 'nothing' is another's version of doing 'something'. Here, we have a person with a jam-packed diary for their week, filled with work and social events. Over there, we see another person envisaging a week featuring very little work and several low-key rest days. Both are doing 'something', despite the latter appearing to be the person doing 'nothing'. Days that are full of activities from morning to night do not equal instant happiness or success, nor do they reflect how much hard work or effort someone is putting into their life.

One person's idea of happiness can be completely different from another's, and that's okay. Some like to fill every minute, have an active social life, rise early, have back-to-back meetings and get a daily workout in, and that's great if it's what makes them happy. Other people love the simple life, preferring nights in to nights out; they love switching off at 5 p.m. and not working on any side hustles; they enjoy weekends pottering around the house and garden and keeping their options open. Some people like a mixture of both of these lifestyles.

I know I have definitely changed over the years. I used to want to fill my time and found it uncomfortable simply being. I associated free time with not being good or successful enough. Free time then meant to me a mediocre social life, a lack of friends, a lack of professional success and a lack of achievement on different levels. Now I absolutely know that this association isn't true in any form or sense, and I love my stillness and free time when I have them. I embrace both worlds, working with passion and purpose during certain weeks and enjoying doing as much 'nothing' as I can during others.

So, when you see videos or pictures of other people enjoying life and achieving goals, be happy for them, and ensure that what you see doesn't make you question how you are living your life. If it inspires you, that's great, but if it makes you feel bad in any way, then very quickly move past the pictures and the thoughts associated with them. You will see some people always on the go, constantly doing things and achieving things, and that's absolutely fine … for them. But don't let it make you think *What am I doing or achieving in my life?*

Imagine doing things that didn't make you feel good just to be able to share a picture for others to see. Would it be worth it? Imagine a world where sharing pictures or exchanging stories didn't exist: would that relieve the pressure? Would you be more at peace in doing what you want to do rather than what looks good?

There is absolutely no right or wrong way to be, as long as you are happy, being true to yourself, doing things for the right reason, questioning the motives behind your thoughts and actions and not judging others for being different from you. We don't need to label or judge laid-back days as being boring, chaotic, crazy, unproductive or inactive: if it makes us feel good, then the day is GREAT.

Those who want to keep achieving goals and hitting targets need always to question their purpose in doing so. If it simply makes you happy and you enjoy the journey and experience, then great; however, if you are doing it to fill an empty space, to avoid feeling lonely and insecure or to feel worthwhile and accomplished, then you may need to think again and work on some of these deeper issues.

I have worked with many people who were extremely busy in their various roles, often feeling burnt out and exhausted, but continuing to strive like this each and every day in order to feel they were achieving something. Working hard meant that they were a 'somebody', even though people in their past had made them feel like a nobody; it made them feel good enough, despite the fact that people had once made them feel they weren't.

Having recognition, awards and success meant they felt that they were worthy, but if they stopped striving, their confidence, self-esteem and self-worth would evaporate.

I speak to people who fill their diaries with social events, coffee dates and dinners out because it gives them a sense of belonging, a feeling that somebody likes them. They need to be able to say that they went out with friends, colleagues, etc. and that must mean they are good enough. Going out is a good way to boost the ego, to tell others about the great things one may have done or may be doing. It can also be a form of escapism, where the person is avoiding spending time at home or being alone with their thoughts. Keeping busy can often signal avoidance of deeper issues. Those same people can't say no to social events or invitations in case they miss out on something important, in case they get forgotten about next time, in case people stop liking them.

It is important to ensure that keeping busy isn't something you become dependent on in order to remain 'happy'.

It's a natural response to believe that this doesn't affect you, but without judging yourself, take a moment and ask yourself why you do what you do. Are you filling your days because you have a true passion and purpose for what you are working on and enjoy being with others, or are there deeper reasons behind it all? Would having time out for yourself feel uncomfortable to you? Would having a whole free evening or day make you feel alone? Or are you equally happy whether you go out with others or stay in alone?

When I was in the middle of my depression, loneliness was a huge issue. So, if I ever had a day off with nothing or no one to fill it, I saw it as a reflection of my worth. Not having friends to call for a coffee meant I must be unlikeable; the fact that I had just moved to a new town and that making new friends wasn't an instant or easy process never formed part of my reasoning. Not having any major career or personal goals meant I must be inadequate, boring and simply not ambitious or bright enough. The idea of just being content and of taking my time to think about my goals and direction didn't cross my mind at the time. I was trying to crowd my days with activity simply to fill a void: I needed plans and people to assuage my loneliness.

As I worked on myself and the loneliness faded, I absolutely loved days of doing 'nothing'. I loved being in my own company and pottering around the house; even doing the simplest tasks such as the laundry or making a cup of tea gave me so much joy. I was finding joy in the simplest things, feeling content that my body was still mobile and able to do these things, feeling content that I had a home that gave me shelter, feeling content to stare out of the window at the changing seasons.

I also still loved to meet my friends and family, I still loved going out or visiting places, I still worked on my goals – but all this was no longer to fill a void. I was happy in both settings, at home or outdoors, with myself or with others. There really is a huge difference when you do things that truly originate within.

If you happen to know people around you who are content doing their own thing, don't socialise as much as you or don't seem to be working on progressing in their career or in any other area, don't question or judge them. This for them is their goal: simply to be, to feel content exactly where they are.

My parents love to read, go for a walk, watch a little TV, do things around the house, phone their family or have a chat over the fence with their neighbour; they never get bored and often tell me they don't know where the day goes. I used to always try and get them to come and visit places with me, whether it was the local coffee shop or a new city, and as much as they enjoyed doing that, it wasn't a necessity for them. They were just as content doing their own thing at home as spending a little time with us.

I used to need to fill my weekends with activities to feel as if I had done something or so that I could tell myself I had taken the kids out. The kids were content either to stay in or to go out, but the story of taking them out sounded better in my head. Now I let go of those stories and do what feels good to me and us, and sometimes that means a very lazy weekend of doing nothing but lounging, eating, watching a movie, talking and playing games. Sometimes the four of us are happy doing our own things and reuniting at certain parts of the day instead of planning the idyllic 'family weekend'. Sometimes we plan activities for the weekend and sometimes we are super spontaneous, which we also love; for example, we might simply wake up and decide to go to London for breakfast and have a busy, active day there. I embrace doing what feels good and not what looks good.

I remember speaking to parents who had felt like failures after the long summer break because they had seen all the amazing social media pictures of things that other families were getting up to and they felt they hadn't done half as much. They felt they had let their children down, even though their children were perfectly happy. However, they only felt they had let the children down, or felt they hadn't done enough, after looking at other people's pictures and hearing their stories; prior to that, they were having a great summer holiday creating their own fun. Views get warped when we compare our own situations with what 'looks good', and we forget about the pictures and stories that perhaps weren't shared: the broken vehicle, the queues in the theme park, the tired children, the exhausted parents, the extortionate prices, the getting lost en route, etc.

So do what feels good for you, do what makes you feel happy, stay true to your passion and purpose, and if you know there are deeper reasons underlying what you are doing, then take time to acknowledge that and work on it.

The more you focus on your needs and happiness, the less FOMO (fear of missing out) you will experience, the less you will worry what others are doing, and the less impact their life will have on your own. Our time on this planet is short, so spend it doing and discovering the things you love.

Live authentically and in your own lane, and you will see exactly how fulfilling life can be just by living for *YOU*.

Manifestation

Manifestation is not what you want; it is who you are

Over the past few years, the word 'manifestation' has been widely discussed and documented, whether by people reporting how they manifested incredible things in their lives or by people selling courses and guides on manifestation. When you see that somebody has manifested something amazing, of course you want to know how so you can apply that to your own life. We all want incredible things to manifest, right? Especially when people make manifestation look easy and appear so happy in their current lives.

After researching manifestation extensively and applying it to my own life, I can tell you that manifestation is NOT simply wishing for things and hoping for the best; it's not telling the universe your requirements and waiting for it to deliver them overnight or even instantly; it's not just about writing your wishes down or putting them on a vision board and waiting for a knock at the door or for the phone to ring with good news.

The idea of manifestation has roots in various philosophical and spiritual traditions throughout history. While the term 'manifestation' may not have been used explicitly, similar concepts and principles can be found in different cultures and belief systems.

One notable influence on the modern understanding of manifestation is the New Thought movement, which emerged in the late nineteenth century. New Thought philosophers and authors, such as Phineas Quimby, Ralph Waldo Emerson and Mary Baker Eddy, emphasised the power of thoughts, beliefs and the mind in shaping one's reality. They believed that through focused thinking and alignment with the divine, individuals could attract positive experiences and improve their lives.

The idea of manifestation also has ties to ancient wisdom traditions such as Hermeticism, which dates back to ancient Egypt and Greece. The principle of 'as above, so below' and the notion that the mind has the power to create reality are central to Hermetic teachings.

Additionally, the concept of manifestation is reflected in various spiritual and religious practices, including visualisation and prayer. Many belief systems recognise the influence of intention, faith and focused attention in bringing about desired outcomes.

In recent years, the concept of manifestation has gained popularity through books like *The Secret* by Rhonda Byrne, which introduced the idea to a broader audience and emphasised the role of the law of attraction in manifesting one's desires.

Overall, while the specific term 'manifestation' may have gained prominence in more recent times, the underlying principles and ideas have been present in various forms throughout history. The process of manifestation typically involves setting clear intentions, visualising the desired outcome and cultivating positive beliefs and emotions around it.

Manifestation does work, but you still have to do the practical work in many different ways:

1. Put in 100 per cent effort, and work on your goal and dream as much as possible. You still have to take action and steps, have focus and give it your all. For example, if you were trying to give up your current job in order to work for yourself, simply quitting your job and expecting to flourish instantly in your own business would not be a successful strategy. You are manifesting for a successful business, so you need to put in the daily work in for it. Research, build a network, keep going every day. And keep putting the work in. Alongside this, keep your mindset and belief system as positive as possible.

2. You have to surrender to the outcome, and this is often the toughest one to master. We are so very used to wanting outcomes to be ideal, to be in control of them, to know what the end results looks like and to have certainty but all of this changes our energy,

bringing in doubt, fear, and anxiety and impacting our clarity, our focus and ultimately our flow. When energy isn't flowing but rather is disrupted or being forced, the outcome will never be what you desire. So, keep working at it every day as noted in point 1, but surrender to the outcome. Give it 100 per cent intention and work, but have zero expectation; let the universe give you the outcome you desire at the right time and the right place. Trust that everything is working in your favour.

3. When you are manifesting, let the time be right for you. These days, when we want something, we want it yesterday, easily and readily available, and until we obtain it, we crave it, wish for it, think of our incompleteness without it. What you must do instead is trust that the timing is being mapped perfectly for you. You may need more growth or more learning; you may need to cross paths with another person: trust that all that you want will unfold at the right time.

4. Your energy needs to be aligned with your goal. If you are still hurting over things in the past, if you are comparing your life with other people's lives, if you have ill feeling towards other people, if forms of jealousy or anger or envy are surfacing in your mind, then any of these things will impact your flow and manifestation. It is so important that you acknowledge and address these issues and work on them. Only by working on these issues, which are absolutely valid, as

they have been caused by something that occurred during your lifetime, can you heal and move on with a clear flow and energy. Addressing new things whilst still being chained to past events or people will never enable you to fully move on, to fully experience the joy in what you wish for.

5. Beyond what you see in the mirror is a beautiful, powerful source of energy that lies within you. When you peel back the layers and tap into this, your flow and your journey will become abundantly enriched.

Manifestation is a long-term process; IT IS NOT something you can dip into when you feel like it or use simply when you need something. Things can take time to manifest not because you don't deserve them but because it has to happen at the right time with the right flow of energy. You will most likely have to go through some uncomfortable transitions and dig deep inside yourself, explore your beliefs, revisit your past and do much more for manifestation to happen … Yes, all this is important for manifestation because your energy needs to be flowing, and for that to happen, inner peace needs to be found and maintained.

Some of the things that I have manifested have taken ten years to fall into place because, despite me believing I had moved on from certain triggers and people, I hadn't actually fully done so. When I continued with the inner work and truly let go and surrendered, the energy aligned, and my hopes manifested. Sometimes the issues we need to work on are deeply rooted and take time; we want to blame others or look for external fixes, but only when we realise that everything stems from within us can the true work begin.

Some of my hopes and dreams have manifested really quickly even surprising me, and that was because the right energy and intention were there to begin with, the work was being put in, and I felt no pressure or expectation in respect of the outcome; I had surrendered from the get-go.

This is a really random analogy, but I feel it is important to share it. When we eat food or have a drink, our body is good at getting rid of most of the toxic material from it; the things that aren't serving our body's needs we tend to excrete out. Not everything that isn't good for us gets excreted, otherwise we wouldn't have some of the physical illnesses and problems that we do, but the body consistently works hard every day trying to remove waste from itself.

Now think about the words of other people that you hear or see written down, and consider the experiences you've had since the minute you were born. Some of these may cause toxicity within you – the hurt you have felt, the pain you have experienced – but we don't have a system in place that continuously gets rid of these unwanted memories and beliefs from our heart, mind and soul. Instead, we continue to store them, refer to them, and use them to build further beliefs that don't serve us in any way. When your mind and heart are filled with such energy, that isn't healthy nor does it serve your current purpose and future dreams. It will impact your state of flow. We need to consciously work on getting rid of these toxic emotions daily.

I know I mention flow a lot, but it is vital for manifestation. Think about a motorway or a highway where you are driving easily at a good speed but are unexpectedly hit by a traffic hold-up. You are forced to sit in the traffic for ages and it delays your journey, putting you in a bad mood. But suddenly, the obstruction clears, and vehicles are able to flow again; your sudden relief at being able once again to move at a steady pace feels great. When you block your internal flow, your desired outcomes and dreams become delayed too, affecting your mindset. The more in tune you become with yourself, the more you become aware when your energy is blocked. Ever had a day when something doesn't quite feel right? You don't feel great and you are not sure why. Your mood is a little lower than usual. It is important to identify the cause of this issue – the obstruction to your flow – so you can work on it to clear it, allowing your energy to work its magic once again.

As well as clearing obstructions by limiting beliefs and emotions that aren't serving you, it is also important not to force things. Just as a river flows in the direction it needs to, you can flow with the river and have a smooth ride, or you can force yourself against the current believing there are short cuts and be faced with a much more difficult journey. Give your dreams the time, energy, space and flow they requires to work.

Flow becomes easier when you don't add extra pressures and stresses when there are obstructions but do your best in surrendering to what you can't control and focus on what you can; this allows you to continue on your journey with ease. If, instead of swearing, moaning, huffing and puffing, and feeling frustrated by a situation you couldn't control, you had had a few snacks and some water and listened to a podcast or some great music during the delay on the motorway, you would have felt much better.

Have strategies in place when things aren't happening easily or quickly: a go-to self-care list featuring items such as making your favourite meal, going to the movies, journaling, meditating, exercising and lighting a candle. This isn't easy, but if you want to manifest, it's necessary. It may feel uncomfortable to start with, and it may cause low moments and dips in your resolve, but the happiness and peace you experience after using your strategies will be so worth it. You are the only one who can manifest your dream life. ONLY YOU can do it, so if you are in it for the long run, LET'S GET TO WORK.

1. Write down your hopes and dreams clearly and specifically. Write them down even if they seem impossible or unattainable. Don't place any restrictions on them such as 'I can't do that, because I don't have the time' or 'I can't achieve that – I don't have enough money'; imagine everything is possible and available and write them all down. If you like, you can add pictures next to your writing to create a vision board. Have this in a place where you can see it every day; this will help keep your mind focused and working towards the dream.

2. If you are into crystals and incense, you can mark this moment by meditating with a crystal and lighting incense or using some sage to clear the energy around you. I won't be going too much into crystals and incense, as they're a personal and optional choice, and I am certainly not expert enough about them to share anything more than basic information.

3. Now we dig deep. Take a moment to look at your life patterns. What beliefs or thoughts have often held you back? Which people or scenarios keep triggering your emotions? What feelings and thoughts do they provoke? What or who doesn't make you feel so good? It is so important to begin to frame these answers; some may be obvious and others less so. Write them all down, and even if your response seems small or insignificant, write it anyway. The more you acknowledge and face your past, the clearer your energy for the future will be. Remember that the scenario or person can't control you unless you choose to let that happen. Even though you are tempted to blame a particular person or circumstance, and with good reason, IT DOESN'T MATTER. As harsh as that may sound, it really doesn't matter. It's you that has to change. So choose you over that person or circumstance right now. Have a conversation with yourself: yes, once upon a time you were impacted by a certain person or scenario, but that's not you any more; you no longer choose to be impacted and instead look forward to a life of peace and happiness. You choose

flow over fear or frustration. You choose happiness over sadness. You choose to let it go. Certain issues may be deeply rooted, and you may choose this point to ask a professional or your GP to work with you in addressing and overcoming these. Clearing the beliefs that no longer serve you, resetting your mindset and unblocking areas that cause emotional triggers are vital steps and a huge part of manifestation. When you work on this, you will feel a weight being lifted; you will feel a sense of ease and peace.

4. Begin working on your dreams every single day, and start the journey. You may say, 'Sheena, I want a new house and a new partner, and I want to become rich. How can I work on that?' You can work on, and have, all of those things; you just can't expect them to appear magically overnight. Think about why you want some of these things. Which aspect of having them do you think will make you happy? Does ego come into play at any point? Do you think having a partner will make you feel whole? Your reason, motive and purpose have to be genuine and expressed with good intention. The more authentic and genuine you are, the better your flow will be. As you work on yourself, you may realise you don't actually want some of these things.

5. Start assessing your current situation and reality. If, for example, your ambition is to have a new house, look at your finances, consider what you need in a new house, take a look at houses and areas that are available to

you. Do you need to do some extra overtime, work on a side business, work on saving a little more each month? Focus on what you can do today to get to where you want to be. Work on limiting beliefs, and let go of any fear or doubt about not achieving or getting those things. Keep taking as many steps as you can to work on your goal. Keep working on practical steps to ensure that you move forward.

6. Keep working with 100 per cent intention and 0 per cent expectation; surrender to the outcome. The universe knows what you want, and now you have to trust in its timing of delivery or wait for it to reveal an even better path for you. It may take a while, it may change your desires, it may show you something entirely new, but as you surrender, the plan will slowly unfold – just trust that it will be to your ultimate benefit.

7. Pay attention to opportunities that arise, and take inspired, purposeful steps towards your goal. The universe responds to your intentions and efforts, so be proactive, and seize the opportunities that come your way. If we focus on things that aren't going right, then we can easily miss the wonderful opportunities that present themselves.

8. Continue to cultivate positive beliefs and emotions around your desired outcome. Believe that it is possible for you to manifest it, and let go of any doubts

or limiting beliefs that may arise. Embody the feelings of already having achieved your goal, feelings such as gratitude, joy and excitement. Use positive affirmations, journaling and meditation to continue to embed the beliefs in your subconscious mindset so that your mind is working towards supporting your dreams.

Remember that manifestation is a personal and subjective process, and what works for one person may not work the same way for another. Experiment with these tips, adapt them to suit your needs, and find what resonates with you the most. Stay consistent, stay focused, and trust in your ability to manifest your desires.

Inner thoughts and inner peace

Our mind and thoughts are either focused on our problems or on finding ways to be happier; after all, the ultimate goal of the brain is to seek happiness. Let's take your day so far as an example. How many times have you thought about your stresses and worries? How many times have you thought about all the things you need to do or should have done? How many times have your failures or thoughts of not being enough crossed your mind? Now think about how many times your thoughts have turned to gratitude or to things that have gone well or to things that are great just by simply existing. Your mind has probably thought more about the problems in your day than about the positive things. The brain thinks about problems because it is trying to find a solution them so you can be happy again, and when it's not doing that, it's constantly scanning the world for things that it thinks will make you happier: a better work–life balance, that new restaurant that's opened, the holiday destination you heard your friend went to, that dream dress for your wedding, etc.

It's important we learn to truly love simply being. Think about this: when you have a headache, a stomach ache, a cold or another health issue, do you then appreciate what it felt like to have good health before the onset of your illness? Do you then remember when your body was just being, delivering to your requirements, giving you what you needed when you needed it with wonderful energy? You were able to enjoy your day without the physical pain and tiredness your body is now giving you.

What about taking time to appreciate and love being where you are right now? If you are fortunate enough to currently be in good health, how about taking time to acknowledge that? Take time to appreciate your wonderful senses that allow you to enjoy the surrounding world and experience it.

We give a lot of energy and thought to times when we are hungry, when we are cold, when we need something, but what about giving the same energy and thought, if not more, to times when our needs are already met. We don't tend to think *Oh, how wonderful to be in a home that's giving me shelter and warmth*, or *There is so much choice and availability of foods to nourish me in my fridge and cupboards*. We simply accept those situations.

How about we now start putting more of our energy into the things we have rather than what we don't have? Let's start releasing the extra negative energy, thoughts and stories that we add to our daily problems. It's not about ignoring our worries but rather observing the situation and then moving forward productively.

For example, your daily worries might include having lots of chores – laundry, ironing, cooking, etc. – and being too busy for it all. You could think about the ironing piling up – you never seem to get on top of it and dislike doing it – and how you just aren't great at staying organised. The stories and emotions keep on adding up and your mood continues to become lower; your energy fades and you give up, ending the day not feeling good enough.

How about instead of doing that, you simply lay out and observe the facts? There is ironing that needs to be done. I am going to do it at 8 p.m. whilst watching TV or listening to a podcast, and I'll do what I can for half an hour. Or, there is ironing that requires doing. I am going to do it on Thursday when I have the evening free; it needs to be done as I require clothes to wear for the following week, and I am going to make it as enjoyable as I can by listening to music or my audio book. It's okay that the ironing has built up; I had a busy week, and it doesn't reflect on my organisation or domestic abilities; it's simply a job that needs doing, and I will do it.

Your happiness doesn't depend on your domestic abilities. We can frame this positively by saying that we get to iron clothes ready for our work, an occupation that supports our living and our lifestyle.

Let's begin to release each worry and problem. As you well know, when we extinguish one worry another one tends to surface. Again, this is the brain's way of trying to protect us; it has been subconsciously programmed to inform us of potential worries and fears so that we can do whatever we can to control them, avoid them or get ready to face them. However, we need to start reminding the brain that we don't need these warnings at such an intense level every second of every day.

Of course, if there are imminent dangers and threats, we need to be ready and alert to deal with them, but we don't need the same analytical coping system for all daily worries. We can start to programme our minds to release them and let them go.

If you break a cup in the morning, if the cashier is rude to you, if a family member doesn't give you a compliment, if you don't get that job promotion, then observe your thoughts and emotions and slowly begin to let any negative parts of them go. Let them go as quickly as you can; this will be hard and take practice, but over time, if you keep up with the daily practice, your response time in letting them go will get quicker. Your heart and mind are like magnets: the more you focus on the situation, the more emotion your heart will attract. The quicker you let it go, the less impact it will have on you and the more quickly you will be able to continue with your day.

Move towards the recovery phase as soon as you can; don't take things personally, and see what you can do to move forward instead. Clean up that cup, recognise that maybe the cashier is busy, give yourself a compliment instead, get feedback and work for another promotion.

It all sounds simple, and I am sure there will be a lot of buts incoming, but it really can be that simple especially in terms of your emotions. You don't have to carry that big weight around with you all day, telling yourself your people are never proud of you, telling yourself you are no good at your job, telling yourself you are clumsy, telling yourself your friend doesn't like you, questioning everything and allowing yourself to be consumed by your concerns once more.

THIS WON'T BE EASY, BUT YOU CAN ABSOLUTELY DO IT.

Think about it: you have spent years living and thinking this way; you can't expect to undo all that overnight, but you can absolutely start the journey ... right now. The situations may remain the same, but your perception of them can change. By changing your thoughts, you are changing your responses and actions and living a more peaceful life.

Start stripping away the exterior world, then take away the layers of identity you have created and continue to create for yourself, and start consciously connecting to this powerful inner world where there really is an infinite energy of unconditional bliss. Take away the requirement of needing the identity of a mum, a call centre worker, a sibling, a homeowner, a vegetarian, a sporty type, a creative person, etc. Work on connecting to your inner being, your soul and your pure energy, and notice how incredible the realisation or awakening begins to feel.

You have so much more control over your life and happiness than you realise; however, I am hoping that after reading this book, you will realise this much more vividly than when you started ... and actually believe it too.

Expect the unexpected

When has life ever really gone to plan? Whether it's small bumps along the way or major ones, there will usually be some sort of unexpected moments during the journey. Yet we tend to assume each and every time that the journey will be smooth, and we become disappointed when it isn't.

When you are driving your usual route, is the journey the same every time? The road may be, but the traffic, the scenery, the roadworks, etc. will vary each time.

Maybe you've gone to the airport only to find that your flight is delayed or cancelled; maybe your holiday hotel room isn't what you imagined or has some faults. Or maybe you've gone to the supermarket with a list of ingredients for your favourite cake that you've been looking forward to making all week and the supermarket has run out of one of your key ingredients.

When you've planned an event, how many times have things changed or adaptations been necessary? Maybe the caterer didn't have the right menu for you, maybe the venue had issues, maybe the guest list kept changing.

Maybe you've had a sure win on a house you've been after or a job promotion, and at the last minute things fall through. Or maybe you've been in a long-term relationship where things appear to be going well and you see a future, marriage and a family but then something has changed for your partner, or a difficult situation has arisen, and the relationship has broken down. It's a scenario you never imagined or expected.

These scenarios may sound gloomy, but they're definitely not meant to be; instead, they are intended to highlight that the unexpected happens all the time, no matter how detailed and precise our plans are. And that's okay. We as humans are more adaptable and resilient than we realise or give ourselves credit for.

Expecting the unexpected doesn't mean you aren't being hopeful or optimistic; it means you are giving situations your very best effort, and by expecting the unexpected you will be less consumed by the setback and be able to turn your attention more quickly to your recovery and response.

Instead of going to the supermarket and feeling disappointed that the ingredient for your desert isn't there and cursing your luck or feeling frustrated, let go of those emotions more quickly and devise an alternative solution to the problem, perhaps thinking of a different dessert to make, looking for a substitute ingredient, checking when it will be available again or if it's in stock at the back of the store, or trying a different shop.

I'm also not saying go into a relationship with doubt and the expectation of breaking up at the back of your mind; rather, I'm saying approach any form of external involvement by investing in yourself first.

Change is the only thing that is guaranteed in the external world, and understanding that is the first step in adapting to it more quickly.

Take a moment to think about some of the things, small or big, that have changed or been unexpected in your past. How did you react or respond? Did it take you some time?

One of the moments that springs to my mind as I type this is the time I ordered a cake for my daughter. She was obsessed with the colour pink at the time, and when the cake turned up, it was yellow. My initial thought was *Wow! The cake looks pretty, but oh my gosh, my daughter might not take this very well*. Thoughts of making a mad dash to get an additional pink cake came to mind, but then I took a few breaths and thought: *It's a beautiful cake. The colour was an error, and the cake maker is devastated, but in the grand scheme of things, it really doesn't matter.* It was a Beauty and the Beast cake, so I could tell my daughter that Belle's favourite colour was yellow and it was so much more magical to have that on her cake. And when I eventually unveiled her cake, she wasn't even fazed, nor did she query the colour. It was a humorous moment now etched in my birthday-drama memories!

Now, that was a very small moment; there have been many changes and unanticipated events in my life: changes of job when I had originally thought that I would be at a certain place for a long time; changes of school; an unexpected C-section; people leaving my life. Small changes and big changes occur in all our lives; some of them we plan, and some are very much unexpected. We now need to understand that, despite all our planning, the unexpected always arises, and we need to be mindset-ready for it. It no longer needs to shock or overwhelm us for days: we can respond to it, take it on, manage it and still move forward.

One of the hardest unexpected situations to deal with is the death of someone close. Bereavement can trigger a vast range of emotions, some of which will depend on the nature of our relationship with the person who has died and any unresolved issues with them that might exist in our mind. Attachment and detachment play an important role: accepting the process and cycle of life, appreciating the value that person brought into your life, understanding any lessons they taught you on your own journey and then, over time, learning to let go of any pain.

There may be people who hurt you and have now departed, and you may not have had the chance to speak to them, or you may feel they never knew the hurt they inflicted on you, and now you feel lost in the emotion of that situation. Journaling and writing a letter to that person can certainly be the first step in the healing process. Their physical presence may have left the world, but ensure that their mental presence leaves your world too so you can continue to live peacefully within yourself.

As for the loved ones that leave us, know that time will heal and that their presence left a beautiful imprint on your heart, but recognise that we are all souls on a journey. Their soul is continuing its journey, and you can take everything good that you felt in, and learnt from, your relationship and continue with your own journey.

Life is full of surprises, so work on not becoming too elevated in happiness or too depressed in pain. You will feel highs and lows with equal intensity, but when your mind is in a state of equanimity, you will be able to observe and experience these moments without being consumed by them. Feel the inner gratitude and inner happiness when things go well; acknowledge the feelings when things don't work out; but above all, continue to keep working on moving forwards. You are exactly where you are meant to be in this moment in time. Don't allow that fact to be an excuse for procrastination; use it instead to provide you with the motivation to keep going.

With every situation in life, when you develop and deepen your inner peace and happiness, the outer world will faze you less and less.

Positive affirmations

Every thought we have causes a physical change in our body, impacting our emotions and mood. Repetitious thinking of certain thoughts has been found to change our neural pathways and change the structure of our brain so that it can serve us better.

Positive statements and suggestions can really influence and impact how you feel, behave and live. Affirmations are statements that can support you in your journey. They help you feel positive, encouraged, calm and motivated.

The brain uses images and words to function, feel and deliver, so when you make a positive affirmation and accompany it with a related image, it can be very powerful. If I were to say, 'I am relaxed' or 'I am calm' and visualise a beach or a desert island, then my brain would start working towards this image, and do everything possible to enhance it, giving me the feeling of being calm and relaxed. This can help when you may be feeling anxious before an exam or a presentation, or just in your general day-to-day life.

When you make negative affirmations, usually at the end of a busy day or week, you may say things such as 'I am tired', 'I am overworked', 'I am stressed' or 'I am overwhelmed'. Your brain will receive these messages and begin to respond. You may feel more tired and you may lose motivation, or you may become physically ill, because your brain thinks it's trying to help you by making you slow down so that you stop to reset. But you need to stop, reset and recharge before you get to this stage. Have you ever been ill at home, telling yourself 'I feel ill' over and over as you snuggle further and further under a duvet feeling not so great? If so, you might have noticed that as soon as you have a shower or move around a little so that you are distracted from your own dialogue, you actually start to feel better.

I remember speaking to a client who had a health scare and was waiting for certain tests to give him official results. During this waiting period of a couple of weeks, my client felt unwell; he kept telling himself something must be wrong, and therefore, he physically felt symptoms of illness. He felt run-down and lost his energy; his brain was telling him that if he was unwell, it would support him by slowing him down. Then came his results, which showed everything was clear, healthy and normal, and suddenly he felt fit as a fiddle and had more energy, and that weight was lifted from his shoulders. The power of his own words and the images he had created were what had held him back, not any real physical illness.

Affirmations are also known to activate the reward centres in the brain and release chemicals such as dopamine, which can really help us when we're feeling low, demotivated or stressed. Research has also shown it to increase activity in other areas of the brain known to process and help regulate any negative information or emotion.

Affirmations can help you in a range of ways.

1. They can help you to improve your physical health by reprogramming the subconscious mind: affirmations aim to rewire the subconscious mind, which holds deep-rooted beliefs and patterns. By repeating positive statements, you can gradually replace negative or limiting beliefs with more empowering ones. This process helps to shift your mindset towards a more positive and self-supportive outlook.

2. Affirmations redirect your focus and attention towards positive aspects of yourself and your life. They help you to become aware of your strengths, capabilities and potential. By consistently affirming positive statements, you train your mind to pay attention to the positive aspects and opportunities around you.

3. Affirmations are not only about the words you say or think; they also evoke emotions. When you repeat positive affirmations, you generate positive emotions such as joy, confidence and gratitude. These emotions have a direct impact on your overall well-being and can enhance your motivation and resilience.

4. Affirmations boost your self-belief and confidence. As you repeat affirmations that reinforce positive qualities, abilities and outcomes, you start to develop a stronger belief in yourself and your abilities. This increased self-confidence can lead to taking bolder actions, pursuing your goals with conviction and attracting positive experiences.

5. Affirmations serve as a counterbalance to negative self-talk and self-doubt. They help to challenge and replace negative thoughts and beliefs that hold you back. By consistently practising affirmations, you create a mental shift that allows you to silence self-criticism and cultivate self-compassion.

6. Affirmations reduce stress and anxiety and improve self-worth, self-esteem and self-confidence.

How to say affirmations

You can say positive affirmations at any time of the day. I usually like to say them at the start of my day and then come back to them later if I need to. Your affirmations can be anything you want and can be unique to you and support what you need that moment, that day or that week. Say them in your mind or ideally out loud, as this can feel really empowering and uplifting too. Keep it a consistent practice, setting aside five minutes a day to focus on it.

Affirmations should be said in the present tense because your brain doesn't recognise past or future; it believes everything is happening in present time. When you repeat an affirmation to yourself, it believes you are already feeling it and being it and will try to support you in every way to achieve it.

When you are watching a thriller movie, does your heart start beating faster at a particularly suspenseful scene? Do you feel nervous? Do you become scared? Do you feel all those things despite the fact that you are sitting at home and none of them are actually happening to you? This is because your brain believes all these things *are* happening to you; it believes the movie is part of your life.

Visualise a big, bright yellow lemon and imagine cutting this lemon in half, seeing the juice squirting out of it as you cut it. Now imagine placing a slice of this big, fresh, juicy lemon into your mouth and letting the flavour explode, allowing the juice of the lemon to cover your tongue ... Do you notice you start salivating? Do you start actually tasting the lemon? That's because the brain believes you are eating that lemon right now – all through the power of words and images. The mind is a powerful tool, and it really can turn thoughts into actions and then into reality.

Repeat your affirmations at least five times.

Associate an image with your affirmation if you can.

Be patient, and trust that you are supporting your journey.

Remember that with everything I am teaching you, there are no overnight fixes; rather, it is all to support you in your journey. Saying a positive affirmation won't stop you feeling anxious overnight, or make you feel calm instantaneously, but it will initiate the journey that will get you there. It will get you to where you want to be more quickly each time, and it will enable you to change your thoughts positively much faster, so practise every day or as much as you can. Just like the Couch to 5K programme that you see people doing, it involves small changes and small steps to get to the ultimate goal. If you have never run before, it is very difficult to run five kilometres without following the preparatory steps of the programme (trust me, I've tried), and if you do, you will definitely notice that it's a struggle; you probably won't feel like doing it again, and the joy will be lost. Consistency and developing strength over time are key, and of course this applies equally to your mental and physical health.

Keep putting the physical work in along with your affirmations. For example, telling yourself 'I am fit and nourished' won't automatically make you feel fit and nourished; you still need to plan a workout and get the nutrients into your body. The affirmation will support your desire and motivation, and over time, working out and eating healthily will become habits and natural parts of your routine.

It is also important to reflect on your limiting beliefs, your past and your values to help support your affirmation work. If you don't truly believe the affirmations you are saying, then they serve no purpose. If you are saying 'I am confident' but really don't believe it, it's important to process where that limiting belief came from and look at reframing your thoughts.

An example of reframing would be changing your thought from *I am not confident in a social setting* to *I am getting better and better every time I go to social events. I am a good listener, and my communication and engagement are improving each time*. The affirmation then could be 'I am great in social settings', and over time, it could become 'I am confident'.

Perhaps you want to be mentally stronger. If you don't believe you can say 'I am strong', you can start by saying 'I am becoming stronger every day'. It's important you align with your affirmations.

Below are some examples of affirmations that you can use, but feel free to create your own.

- I am supported
- I am loved
- I am worthy
- I am peaceful
- I am energised
- I am nourished and healthy
- I am amazing
- I am living in the moment
- I am grateful
- I am beautiful
- I am motivated
- I am doing this
- I am great at speaking

- I am great at socialising
- I am clear and concise in my words and presentations
- I am full of knowledge
- I am learning and growing
- I am excited at the changes in my life
- I am embracing my perfectly imperfect life
- I am enough

Whenever you are having doubts again, you can reframe your thoughts into positive affirmations:

I am the worst tennis player in this group can become 'I am excited to keep improving my skills'.

I am scared to try the new yoga class; everyone will judge me can become 'I am proud of myself for trying something new and giving this gift to support my body'.

I can't stand and do a presentation can become 'I am excited to share my knowledge, and my passion will shine through'.

I am afraid that I will feel inadequate in this new venture can become 'I am proud of myself and ready to make this dream a reality'.

So many times, when these situations have arisen for me and my doubts have crept in, I have told myself 'I am giving it my best, and that is enough' or 'I am learning and will get better each time' or 'I am surrounding myself only with supportive people'.

Once, I was doing some Zoom presentations and had to use some extra functions to make the presentation interactive. It was something new that I had to learn, and it was making me panic slightly. All I knew was that this was an incredible opportunity I had been given, and even if it turned out to be terrible, I wanted to know that I had given it my absolute best shot. I learnt, I watched YouTube videos, I googled for ideas and lessons. I did whatever it took to prepare as effectively as I could, and the end result and feedback were amazing, but most of all, it was important that I didn't give up, didn't say I couldn't do it or wouldn't even try. Instead, I told myself 'I am doing this', 'I am making it happen', 'I am excited at learning something new', 'I am grateful for the opportunity'. I know that everyone starts from somewhere; you've just got to take that first step. The second time you do something new and challenging, it becomes much easier, something I'm sure many of you have experienced too.

Well-being exercise

I want you to set a timer for 20 seconds.

Next, I want you to give yourself the biggest smile you possibly can.

Keep smiling and radiating that joy.

Think about all the amazing things that make you smile and feel happy.

Keep smiling until the 20 seconds are up.

Ideally, do this with your eyes closed.

What do you notice after the 20 seconds?

Do you feel a little happier than you did before?

Do you feel lighter or uplifted?

Do you feel less tense and anxious?

By smiling, you were telling your brain you were happy; your brain believed you and supported this by releasing happy chemicals, giving you a further sense of joy and calm.

The same will happen when you give yourself wonderful uplifting and inspiring affirmations.

Gratitude

The power of practising gratitude is huge; it can really change the perception of your life and how you feel at the end of each day, each week and each month.

Sometimes we only think about gratitude when we achieve something or when something goes our way or to plan. However, it's just as important, if not more so, to practise gratitude on our darkest days and through our deepest fears.

Think about practising gratitude when you are reflecting on your past, when you are anxious about your future and when you are being present in the moment. Through gratitude, your anxieties and worries reduce or fade away. Through gratitude, you realise how far you have come, how strong and resilient you already are and how you can trust in your journey into the unknown future.

When you reflect on the past, think about the lessons you have learnt, how much you have grown personally, how much you have achieved and how far you have come ... because you *have* come so far. You may have encountered hard times and trauma, and you may need to still process these, but you are still here, still showing up, still trying – and that shows courage, strength and resilience. You also know you want better for you, you want change, and you want to achieve your dreams and visions; again, that shows determination, commitment and grit. It may not always feel like you have these characteristics, but YOU DO, and it's important to appreciate yourself and to feel gratitude for yourself and your journey so far.

When you think about the future, it can cause fear and anxiety because it is unknown and uncertain. However, think about it as an exciting journey, where you embrace the perfectly imperfect path and where there is so much to see, hear and experience. There will be ups and downs, but you've got this just like you always have. You don't have to have it all figured out or have all the answers; just know they will unfold in the right time.

You can make one-year, five-year, maybe ten-year plans and goals. I think it is so important to look back one, three, five years or more and look at how far you have come. We always have a habit of thinking that we need to be more and do more, that what we are doing isn't enough or that we have a long way to go, but look at the journey you've covered, the mountains you've climbed, the storms you've battled through to get here. Look at all the small things and the big things you've done: your character has evolved, you've acquired new skills, you've travelled, you've made new friends, you've changed jobs and homes, you've learnt to manage finances, you've become more kind and selfless. Take a moment to look back. You may not think it's a lot, but when you really look, you'll see just how much you've accomplished.

I started noticing how far I had come when I happened to look at old videos we had taken on holidays. I used to be painfully shy and hated the camera; I didn't realise how much I had changed until I saw those videos and compared my reticence in them with my confidence over the last few years during which I have done endless public speaking.

When you think about today – whatever the time is and however your day has been – can you think of any things you are grateful for? What are the simple things that have supported you or made you smile or brought you a little joy and comfort?

Those things could be a person, a place, an acknowledgment, a meal, an object: absolutely anything. The comfort of your home, your bed, your sofa, your books, your TV, your music. Maybe someone was kind, a neighbour smiled, the cashier in the supermarket was friendly, a colleague was complimentary, a partner texted to check in with you. Maybe you had your favourite snack, enjoyed your morning coffee, had a delightful meal. Look around your space and remember every detail of your day and the parts of it that you can feel grateful for, no matter how small. Sometimes the simplest things are the biggest things; sometimes the things right in front of us are the things we need reminding of. As I sit here typing, I am grateful for this laptop allowing me a place to write; as I look around, I am grateful for this room for giving me space to be creative. I am grateful for the hot drink that I savour with each sip.

Okay, so you've thought of some things that you are grateful for. Now what do you do? Take a moment to sit with them, absorb them and see how they make you feel. Writing down your thoughts also really helps, and I recommend the practice of writing down what you're grateful for in a journal every day or every few days or once a week. Write down what you are grateful for and why you are grateful for it.

This is also a nice activity to do with someone, whether it's your partner, a friend or a family member. Sharing gratitude is a really beautiful thing; it's so lovely hearing what other people are grateful for and finding out how they view and see things. It can really open up our own world and make us think about things we may not have or things that we may have forgotten. It's especially great to do this with children, as their view of the world can be so different and refreshing.

There will be setbacks as days go by and challenges on our journey. We are very quick to criticise and judge ourselves and often believe we will be grateful when a certain task is ticked off or when the obstacle in front of us is removed.

By practising gratitude regularly, you will start to naturally look at things more positively. Embrace those days when things go wrong or you have setbacks, and look for the positives in each day to keep you focused, uplifted and motivated. By filling yourself up with gratitude you will be much more content and at peace from within. You are grateful for all that you have and less concerned with what hasn't yet come your way. You are grateful for the now and not living in a regretful past or an anxious future.

Now, I understand how hard it is to feel grateful when you are going through a hard time, and when people suggest being grateful, it can often make you feel guilty of your thoughts or your situation. Trust me, I understand. I've often been told things like this: 'But you have so much to be grateful for! How can you feel down?' or this: 'Life will get better – think about all the amazing things you have.' The hardest thing to hear was this: 'You have so much to be thankful for. Think about all the homeless people or those who are worse off than you.' This made me feel bad for feeling the way I did. I felt guilty instead of grateful.

There are successful, wealthy people, with seemingly perfect relationships, who struggle to say they are feeling down or low because they know they will be judged and questioned and told that they have it all and so can't possibly be down; it's almost as if they don't have the right to feel anything but gratitude and happiness.

Having a lifestyle characterised by material wealth doesn't always equate to pure happiness; there will still be struggles and setbacks where life hurts and disappoints you. You never have to feel guilty for feeling anything you do; everything you feel is valid. So, whether you are a famous celebrity, a parent, a teacher, a lorry driver or a rock star, your role and title have no relevance to your true happiness. You might be going through a break-up, heartache or a change in circumstance; your plans might be in disarray; you might have been let down by someone; but whatever your problem is and whatever your role in life is, it's valid for you to feel all your emotions. You are human just like your neighbour.

Gratitude has to come from you. You have to understand the importance of gratitude to feel it and practise it. By doing so, you can then use it as a daily practice, especially when things in your life aren't going the way you want.

When you practise gratitude, try not to add requirements to it, such as feeling grateful for your car but wishing it had electric windows, or being grateful for your holiday but wishing you were going for two weeks rather than one. Pure gratitude for what you have connects you to an inner peace, to a sense of what you have being enough, with anything else being a bonus. This gratitude actually supports manifestation because you start to feel appreciative in the moment; there are no fears or low vibrations in your mind and body, and therefore the things you are still aiming for start to flow naturally.

When everything is taken away from you, all you have left is yourself and gratitude, and by being grateful for the simplest of things, you will feel that everything else is just a bonus and not a necessity.

Think about your breath and how it helps you to live and experience the world each and every day. Notice your breath going in and out easily and effortlessly to support you and allow you to be here. Your beautiful breath that gives life to everything inside of you so that you can experience everything in the outside world. Simply give thanks to your breath and your body for serving you, enabling you to do so many things, allowing you to experience the world through your senses, allowing you to read these words, to sit wherever you are, to hear the sounds around you, to feel all that you are.

Then, think about some of the things that are important to you, no matter how small or big. There's no right-or-wrong rule here; just think about whatever springs to mind, whether that's your family or that donut you just ate, whether it's your car or the great date you had last night, whether it's your amazing office or the coffee you just drank, whether it's the sun or your home. Think about why you are grateful for these things. What joy or happiness do they bring you? Go a little deeper with your answer: if you could really describe each thing in a paragraph to me, what would you say? How do those things make you feel, and why?

For example, I am grateful for my daughters because they give me so much love and joy; they have enabled me to experience a deep love that I never knew existed. They teach me a new thing every day, whether that's the answer to a maths question or something about their characters. They both teach me how to be present and have more fun, and also how to be patient and kind. I am grateful for my morning coffee because I look forward to starting my day with it; I love the taste and the aroma, and it simply makes me feel good. I am grateful for my home because it gives me shelter; it gives me a place to eat, sleep and sit; and it gives me so much comfort. It gives me the space to feel secure and somewhere to call home – a home filled with memories.

Take a moment to think about how it would feel if you didn't have the things you're grateful for; this may deepen your gratitude for them.

Gratitude can improve relationships and connections, and expressing gratitude towards others strengthens relationships and fosters a sense of connection. When we acknowledge and appreciate the kindness and support of others, it deepens our relationships and promotes a positive social environment. Gratitude helps cultivate empathy, compassion and a sense of reciprocity in our interactions with others.

When you practise gratitude, you begin to perceive things with compassion, you begin to see the positives in any situation, you begin to focus on the good over the bad no matter how small the good may seem. By placing your energy on these positives instead of the negative you are attracting more positives into your life. It stops you from giving up, it keeps you focused, it brings you hope, it keeps you motivated to keep trying, and the flow of energy behind you will ensure that you move in the right direction.

Ultimately, the purpose of practising gratitude is to cultivate a mindset of appreciation, positivity and well-being. It allows us to embrace the present moment, cherish the good in our lives, and foster deeper connections with others. Gratitude practice is a simple yet powerful tool that can positively impact our mental, emotional and physical well-being.

Well-being exercise

Write it down

Use a blank sheet of paper and some bright colours.

1. Write down five things you are grateful for.
2. Write down why you are grateful for each thing (think about what it makes you feel, how it supports you, the purpose it plays in your life).
3. Write down how you would feel if you didn't have those things in your life.
4. If extra things pop into your head, keep adding them to your list.

Share your gratitude with family or a friend

Over a meal or coffee, talk about the things you are grateful for; listen to the people around you and their thoughts about gratitude. Listen to their views and opinions; they may give you a different perspective on things. Then share your views on the things you are grateful for.

Keep a gratitude jar

Find a spare jar. Every time you feel grateful for something, write it on a little bit of paper and pop it in the jar, and every three or six months, have a look at all the things you were grateful for. It's easy to forget all the small moments that made us happy, and sometimes the setbacks and their associated emotions remain more strongly in our minds. So, having these reminders and remembering the good times will continue to shift your mindset towards gratitude and all the things you have rather than the things you lack.

When I was going through some stressful moments, I pulled out some of the things I was grateful for from our jar. These included reminders of some amazing people we had met on holiday who really went above and beyond for us; waking up at 6 a.m. with my eight-year-old to rehearse for her drama exam and having a moment sharing a herbal tea before we began, just the two us; and sitting in the comfort of my lounge reading a new book I had bought whilst the rain fell heavy outside.

This gave me some grounding, it helped change my stressed mode to a grateful one, and it made me feel that I could carry on with a clearer, more positive outlook. It was a reminder that I have so much and that going forward, I'll have opportunities to add new memories to my store.

Gratitude journal

Keep a daily gratitude journal and write down one, two or three things that have made you smile. What made you feel good or brought you joy or gave you peace in your day? It can be absolutely anything: having a pleasant chat with a neighbour, a nice coffee, a smooth commute, a discount on your favourite food purchase, a text message.

Meditation

Meditation is something that changed a lot of things for me. It was a huge part of my personal growth and transformation, and it is a practice that I still include in my daily life as I continue my journey. When I first started the practice, I had no idea what to do and no idea what to expect; I had no guarantee of experiencing any benefits. All I knew was it was something I wanted to try and something that I believed would help me. I was in a place where looking externally for things and people to fuel my happiness wasn't working, and I knew I had to do something else. Meditation seemed a good place to start.

I read up on meditation – what it was and the various forms I could experience and try – and I took some classes to see how it felt. Now, from a very young age, I was always a spiritual person, turning to my faith in times of fear and darkness, and I always had a specific mantra that I used to repeat. I knew that when repeating this mantra, I felt a sense of calm and peace, and I hoped that meditation would enhance or at least support this feeling. When I tried my first class, I was hoping for something miraculous to happen – nothing over the top, but I really wanted it to be the key to what I was searching for, the peace and the connection to myself that I craved. I didn't really feel any of those things. When it was over, people around me spoke of how they loved it, how they felt so light and relaxed. Yes, I felt relaxed, but that wasn't what I wanted. To be honest I didn't know what I felt, other than just not much. However, something told me not to give up, to let go of expectation and try again.

Meditation practice is exactly that … a practice. It cannot be defined by one characteristic, one technique or one method; it really is a progression of many things. It is an unravelling and evolution of the inner self. One of the greatest ways of generating inner peace and raising your vibration stems from meditation. Over time, I practised consistently at home. I didn't create an elaborate meditation area with crystals and candles, etc.; I literally sat on my sofa, focusing on my breathing, and listened to a guided mantra. I finished with a few more moments of focusing on my breathing, with the whole session lasting for a total of twenty minutes. Over time, I noticed such a difference in how I responded to the day afterwards: I felt a beautiful peace inside of me and realised that the things I used to stress about really didn't matter; the ranting and raging mum that I was so used to being was fading. This emotional roller coaster of a person was becoming more stable.

You become awakened to a new sense of alertness; you realise you are not your thoughts but simply an observer of, and witness to, your thoughts. This is one of the most empowering aspects of meditation because you understand that the self, the person within you, is separate from everything external. You realise that things, whether good or bad, are no longer happening to you, but rather around you. The flow of inner peace begins to emerge and deepen, and the stresses, worries and chaos of life begin to fade away. It's as if your mind is a snow globe that's constantly being shaken: the snow resembles your thoughts going in all sorts of directions and bumping into each other, with you often not knowing whether you are coming or going; meditation allows the snow (your thoughts) to settle in the globe (your mind) thus giving you peace.

As your state of alertness heightens, you find that you become very aware of your actions and words and much more mindful in your responses. You begin to choose forgiveness and peace over anger and frustration; you choose giving and letting things go over arguments and greed; you choose being kind and selfless over hurt and anguish. Your authentic self emerges brighter than ever.

You will begin to clear out the negative energies from within, and your vibration will begin to rise.

The key thought I had when starting my meditation journey was not to put any pressure or expectation or judgement on myself. Simply trying for 60 seconds was good enough to begin with; feeling distracted or not understanding what I was meant to feel was okay, as over time, everything would make sense, and the distracting thoughts would become few and far between. As with every new routine, it takes time to become familiar with what works for you and for you to see the results; you wouldn't, for example, expect to see an overnight change after your first visit to the gym.

So, if you are considering trying meditation, let me start by telling you some of the benefits it can bring you.

It reduces stress and anxiety.

It reduces the risk of physical health issues like high blood pressure and heart problems.

It boosts your self-esteem.

It increases your confidence.

It improves your sense of self-worth, your compassion for yourself and your social interactions.

It improves your calm, clarity and focus.

It stimulates theta and alpha brainwaves, promoting a positive mental state and enhanced learning.

Meditation has been shown to have various positive impacts on the brain. Here are some ways in which meditation can influence the brain:

Increased grey matter: Studies have found that long-term meditation practitioners tend to have increased grey matter volume in regions of the brain associated with attention, emotional regulation and self-awareness. This suggests that meditation may support brain plasticity and structural changes.

Strengthened prefrontal cortex: The prefrontal cortex, responsible for executive functions such as decision-making, attention and self-regulation, appears to be influenced by meditation. Regular practice has been associated with a strengthened prefrontal cortex, potentially leading to improved cognitive abilities and emotional regulation.

Enhanced attention and concentration: Meditation practices often involve focused attention on an object, such as the breath or a mantra. This sustained attention training can improve the ability to concentrate and sustain focus in day-to-day activities.

Reduced activity in the default mode network: The default mode network (DMN) is a brain network involved in mind-wandering, self-referential thinking and rumination. Research suggests that meditation can decrease the activation and connectivity within the DMN, which is associated with a quieter mind, reduced self-centred thoughts and enhanced present-moment awareness.

Lowered activity in the amygdala: The amygdala plays a crucial role in processing emotions, particularly fear and stress responses. Meditation has been found to decrease amygdala activity, which can result in reduced reactivity to emotional stimuli and greater emotional resilience.

Increased connectivity across brain networks: Meditation has been associated with increased connectivity between different brain regions and networks. This enhanced connectivity may facilitate better integration of information, improved cognitive flexibility, and a more holistic mode of processing information.

Reduced stress and improved well-being: Meditation practices, such as mindfulness meditation, have been found to lower stress levels and promote overall well-being. These effects are thought to be mediated through changes in brain activity and the regulation of stress-related brain regions.

It's important to note that the effects of meditation can vary among individuals, and the specific brain changes may depend on the type of meditation practice, duration of practice and individual differences. However, research suggests that regular meditation can have positive effects on brain structure, function and emotional well-being.

Incorporating meditation as a regular practice really allows you to become aware of your thoughts, observe your thoughts and be at peace with them instead of being consumed and overwhelmed by them.

There are various types of meditation, each with its own approach and focus. Here are some commonly practised types of meditation.

Mindfulness Meditation: Mindfulness meditation involves cultivating a non-judgemental awareness of the present moment. It typically involves focusing on the breath, bodily sensations or sensations in the surrounding environment. The goal is to observe thoughts, feelings and sensations without getting caught up in them or reacting to them.

Loving Kindness Meditation: Loving kindness meditation, also known as Metta meditation, involves generating feelings of compassion, love and goodwill towards oneself and others. Practitioners typically repeat positive phrases or intentions to cultivate feelings of warmth and benevolence towards oneself, loved ones, neutral individuals and even difficult people.

Transcendental Meditation (TM): Transcendental meditation is a technique that involves the use of a mantra, a specific word or sound, to quiet the mind and attain a state of deep relaxation and inner stillness. It is typically practised for twenty minutes twice a day while sitting comfortably with closed eyes.

Guided Visualisation: Guided visualisation involves following verbal instructions to create vivid mental images and scenes. Practitioners are guided to imagine specific experiences or environments to promote relaxation, stress reduction or personal growth. It can involve imagining a peaceful place, visualising the achievement of goals, or rehearsing desired outcomes.

Confidence Meditation: Confidence meditation involves the repetition of affirmations that promote trust in oneself and increased self-worth, allowing practitioners to internalise an enhanced sense of confidence. Over time, this process can help shift default perspectives towards an abiding trust in one's own intuition and abilities.

Body Scan Meditation: Body scan meditation involves systematically directing attention through different parts of the body, starting from the toes and moving up to the head. The aim is to bring awareness to physical sensations, release tension and develop a deeper mind-body connection.

Zen Meditation (Zazen): Zen meditation is a form of seated meditation often practised in Zen Buddhism. It typically involves sitting in a specific posture, focusing on the breath and observing thoughts and sensations as they arise without attachment or judgement.

Kundalini Meditation: Kundalini meditation combines breathwork, chanting, movement and visualisation to awaken and release energy in the body. It aims to balance and harmonise physical, mental and spiritual aspects, often involving the repetition of specific mantras or chants.

Walking Meditation: Walking meditation involves walking slowly and mindfully, bringing awareness to the sensations in the body and the movement of each step. It can be practised indoors or outdoors, and the focus is on the experience of walking itself.

These are just a few examples of meditation practices, and there are many other variations and techniques available. It's important to find a meditation style that resonates with you and meets your specific needs and preferences. You can explore different types of meditation and experiment to discover which ones work best for you. Please don't go into the practice expecting it to transform your life instantly and bring you sudden bliss, the sensation of levitating or a feeling of complete detachment from the world. This will not happen in your first few minutes of practice (or rather, it may do, but it's very unlikely). As with absolutely any new activity, it takes time and practice; you may in due course experience these things but only as you practise and progress.

You will close your eyes and then quite probably be flooded by a variety of thoughts: today's dinner, your job list, what you have planned for tomorrow, the last conversation you had, etc. That's ALL okay. Simply observe the thoughts, give them no attention and focus back on your practice. Continue this, and over time, you will notice that those thoughts are becoming fewer and further between.

It's natural to feel frustrated when you desire a certain outcome and it doesn't seem to happen. You are taking time out to meditate and hoping it will give you calm and peace, and yet you are still feeling distracted, unable to fully focus or concentrate, and you feel irritation bubbling inside you. It's easy to assume this isn't for you, to give up, to think that you can't do it or that you need a certain mindset to meditate successfully … but I want to remind you that you *can* do it. In fact, if you are initially unsure about meditation, it will probably be of particular benefit to you.

A nice way to start is with a walking meditation. Stand comfortably, link your hands together behind your back so they are not swinging, lower your gaze and walk a few steps forward and backwards slowly. By walking and focusing on the ground ahead of you and on your breath, you are slowly starting to slow the noise of your mind down. Do this for five to ten minutes (longer if you are outside), and then find a spot to sit down, and see if you can do a short seated meditation. This can be a guided meditation via an app, a chant or simply focusing on your breathwork. The walking part of the routine helps us to slow down, which is helpful, as it takes a little longer to quieten the mind down when going into a meditation from another activity.

Remember that you can practise meditation anywhere at any time – it is simply focusing on your breathing and being aware of your thoughts; in more formal meditation, you will set aside a specific period of time for your practice. As always, everything begins with one: one step, one focused breath, one chant, one visualisation.

Monitor and track how you feel. Notice your mood and emotions prior to your practice; keep a mental note of them, perhaps writing them down or giving them a grade on a scale from 1 to 10, and then see if there is a difference after your practice. Again, there is no pressure to see an instant change; just keep tracking yourself each time.

Now let me illustrate in a little more detail two types of meditation techniques from the list above that I find particularly helpful.

Loving kindness meditation

This meditation practises compassion, kindness, love and appreciation for self and others. It is free from any expectation. Buddha said that 'unless we treat ourselves with love and compassion, we cannot reflect the same on others'.

Find a place where you are comfortable and distraction-free.

Sit comfortably on the floor or on a chair, with your hands gently resting on your lap. Keep your spine nice and straight, and try to relax your whole body.

Gently close your eyes or lower your gaze. If any thoughts enter your mind, simply observe them and let them go, giving them no attention.

Take some nice deep breaths in and out.

Take a moment to fill yourself with love, gratitude and appreciation for yourself. Take this time to focus on you and to simply to be.

Now take a moment to think about someone from your past or present who has given you unconditional love. Imagine they are right next to you, telling you all the things that make you amazing and all the things they value and appreciate about you. Allow yourself to feel the love and warmth of this special connection.

As you breathe in and out, allow yourself to relax further and feel loving kindness enter your heart and mind. Imagine this person wishing you happiness and peace, wanting nothing but the best for you.
Use this moment to repeat some affirmations of loving kindness to yourself.

- May I be happy and peaceful
- May I be safe and supported
- May I be healthy and strong
- May I be filled with love and kindness
- I am enough with all I am and have

Repeat these affirmations three times, feeling and believing them each time you say them.

Now think about someone who means a lot to you, someone whom you appreciate and with whom you have a beautiful connection. Now it is time to offer some love and kindness to them. With them in mind, repeat the following affirmations three times:

- May you be happy and peaceful
- May you be safe and supported
- May you be healthy and strong
- May you be filled with love and kindness
- May you feel enough with all that you have and are

Each time you say these affirmations, open your heart, and feel the warmth and love conveyed by your words being received by that individual.

Now think about someone neutral in your life – a colleague, acquaintance or distant friend – and repeat the above affirmations for them too. Wish them well through your words, imagining that, as they receive your thoughts, they feel warm, at ease and peaceful within.

Now imagine someone you have a difficult relationship with, someone who triggers you or is hard to be around, either from your past or in your present. Let go of what they have done or are doing, and see them as an individual with their own battles and struggles. Can you offer them the same good wishes?

As you repeat the words of loving kindness to them, you may notice your own anger and hurt moderating and your heart opening more as you experience a sense of forgiveness and letting go. Take your time and notice what you feel.

Now include all forms of life on this planet: people, plants and animals. Visualise everything and everyone and send them some words of loving kindness:

- May you be happy and peaceful
- May you be safe and supported
- May you be healthy and strong
- May you be filled with love and kindness
- May you feel enough with all that you have and are

Take a moment, and feel this deep love for yourself and all those around you. Feel your heart warming and opening.

Bring your awareness back to the present, take a deep breath, join your hands together, and give yourself some gratitude one more time before gently opening your eyes.

Confidence meditation

Find a space where you can sit comfortably, ideally on the floor with legs crossed and hands resting gently on your lap (comfort is paramount, so use a chair if this is more suitable).

Ensure your spine is straight, as a good, strong posture will enable you to feel positive.

Take a moment to settle in and relax your whole body. Gently lower your gaze or close your eyes. If any thoughts enter your mind, simply observe them and let them go, giving them no attention.

Breathe, and notice your belly expanding as you inhale and contracting as you exhale. Take slow, deep breaths into your belly, and release your breath with slow exhalations.

You will be using three affirmations for each separate inhalation. The affirmations are:

- I am enough
- I am loved
- I am supported

As you breathe in, say 'I am enough', and as you exhale, let go of any doubt and fear.
As you breathe in, say 'I am loved', and as you exhale, let go of any doubt and fear.

As you breathe in, say 'I am supported', and as you exhale, let go of any doubt and fear.

Continue to repeat these affirmations and to really feel them as you say them or out loud or silently to yourself.

Repeat this sequence for as long you wish. Start with five minutes if you are new to meditation, and gradually work up to fifteen minutes if you want to extend your meditation time and it feels right for you.

When you are ready to complete your session, take a deep breath, bring your awareness to the present, and gently open your eyes. Notice how you feel and whether it is any different from when you began.

Meditation

Mindfulness

Mindfulness is very much about being in the present moment, using all your five senses to the maximum and letting go of any regretful thoughts about the past or anxious thoughts about the future. Your objective is to give your full attention and awareness to the present moment. This allows you to be kinder and more patient within yourself and appreciate where you are and who you are in that moment.

We live in a busy, chaotic world, and our emotions and thoughts are changing constantly and quickly. Mindfulness slows this all down so that we can appreciate and value all our experiences, be they simple or complex.

Mindfulness and meditation are interrelated, but there are some differences between them too. John Kabat-Zinn, creator of mindfulness-based stress reduction, defines mindfulness as 'the awareness that arises through paying attention, on purpose, in the present moment, non-judgementally'.

Meditation is often described as the process of focusing on a particular thought, object or pattern of breathing in order to become more aware of oneself, to become calm and to induce a peaceful inner state of being that is indifferent to external events.

Meditation practice can help support an individual in living more mindfully, and mindfulness can enhance meditation.

Mindfulness meditation involves observing one's thoughts and feelings without engaging in them. This can be done anywhere and at any time.

Formal meditation involves specifically taking time out to practise, usually in a seated position and using breathwork as an anchor, intentionally spending a certain amount of time in this practice, whether that's five minutes or an hour or longer.

Mindfulness stops our mind being distracted in various ways and allows us to be present in the current activity. How often do you find yourself eating a meal but thinking about the washing-up, or having a shower and thinking about the day ahead, or watching TV and scrolling on your phone, or talking to someone but thinking about something else? We spend a lot of our time doing one thing while thinking about something else and experiencing the emotions and feelings that continually arise from that duality. Being mindful reduces our stress and anxiety, allows us to think clearly and gives us motivation, and we actually experience things we may have missed before.

Having mindful conversations is really important. Often when we engage in conversation, our mind can drift elsewhere onto the next task we have to do. Sometimes, we listen but only catch some of the conversation because we want to get our point of view or opinion in there. When you have a conversation mindfully, you will learn to let go of distracting thoughts, be fully present, listen to the words you hear and observe the other person's body language. You may notice their expressions or mood changing, which may tell you more than the words they are saying. When it's your turn to speak, be mindful of your own words. Are they coming from a good place? Are you explaining your views as effectively as possible? Are you in a calm mood? A conversation that is mindful can really be very insightful. Albert Mehrabian's 7–38–55 rule states that 7 per cent of meaning is communicated through the spoken word, 38 per cent through tone of voice, and 55 per cent through body language. In other words, only 7 per cent of communication is verbal, with the remaining 93 per cent being non-verbal, so if you are not fully present in a conversation, that will undoubtedly be noticed by the other person.

Here are some of the ways in which you can practise mindfulness.

Mindful senses

Find a space to sit down on the floor or on a chair – either is fine as long as you are comfortable.

Take a moment to take a few deep breaths so you can begin to quieten your thoughts down. Start to let go of any thoughts about the past or the future. If such thoughts enter your mind, simply observe them and then let them go, giving them no further attention.

Now imagine you are seeing your surroundings for the very first time, as if you were an alien who has just landed in this space and has never seen it before (optionally, you can describe what you see in writing).

Five things you can see

Take a look around you, and notice five things you can see. Look above, below and around you. Go a little further, and look at the shapes, textures, sizes and colours of what you notice. Focus on everything you are seeing, letting go of any distracting thoughts.

Four things you can hear

Listen. You may choose to close your eyes as you do so, or close and the open them to notice the effects of doing this on your hearing. What four sounds can you hear? Go a little deeper, and explore the type of sounds you hear. Are they high- or low-pitched, continuous or intermittent, loud or quiet?

Three things you can feel

Think about some of the things you can feel just being as you are. Can you feel the floor or chair you are seated on, the air you are breathing, the clothes you are wearing, any accessories or glasses you may be wearing, the hair on your head? What do these things feel like? Are they hard or soft? Do they cover a large or a small area? Can you feel their texture?

Two things you can smell

What aromas can you smell around you? If this is tricky, you can always light some incense or use a room spray to aid you. Are the smells you are noticing strong or mild? Do they make you think of anything?

One thing you can taste

What can you taste in your mouth right now? Swirl your tongue around: what do you notice?

Becoming absorbed in our senses, letting go of thoughts about the past and the future, allows us to feel calm, still and peaceful. Our 100 per cent focus on the present moment without other distractions allows us to enjoy the experience but also be more mentally productive in the moment. Our thoughts are clearer, our responses are better, our sense of achievement is more fulfilling.

Mindful walking

Next time you go for a walk, instead of simply counting your steps, listening to music, using your phone or thinking about your end destination, start with a few deep breaths. Then once again, let go of any thoughts of the past or the future that may arise. As you begin your walk, start noticing all the wonderful things you can see around you: the trees, the path, the sky, the birds, the people, your feet as they walk. Notice the various shapes and their colours and textures. Look at the buildings and their features: bricks, windows, roofs. Look for interesting markings or colours or anything unique.

Take in the sounds around you: the sound of cars carrying people on their journeys, birds singing, your feet walking, your breathing, the wind or rain as it patters down, people talking, animals moving, leaves rustling.

What do you feel as you continue to walk? It might be the air on your face, your shoes as they hit the ground, your hair being blown across your face, your clothes, the warmth of the sun.

Can you smell or taste anything as you walk? The different seasons can often fill the air with wonderful smells, from blossoming flowers and freshly cut grass to aromas coming from people's kitchens.

At any point in your walk, you can stop, stand still for a minute and focus on one of the senses to enhance it even further.

When you end your walk, notice what was different while you were being more mindful. Did you notice things you'd missed before? Did you feel calmer than usual? Were you able to enjoy the walk more?

Mindful cooking and eating

Everything around us has energy, including the food we prepare and eat. If we are not in a good state of mind, the resultant low energy from us transfers to our food and goes back into our bodies again, lowering our vibration.

When you are preparing and cooking food, be fully mindful. Let go of any other thoughts and distractions, and focus lovingly on the task of cooking. Enjoy the colours and aromas of the ingredients you are using.

When you are eating your meal, ensure that all you are doing is focusing on the task of savouring each mouthful. Try to avoid any distractions, for example, your phone or the TV, and let go of thoughts that are not relevant to the moment, such as the washing-up or jobs that need to be done after dinner.

As you prepare to eat your food, take a moment to look at it. Notice the colours, textures and shapes of the nourishing meal in front of you. You can even go a little further and think about the process of how it got to your plate. Someone has lovingly grown some of the ingredients on your plate, nurtured them, picked them and transported them to the grocery store so that you can then purchase them. The food has come on a long journey to nourish you.

Take a moment to enjoy the aromas of the food, and as you taste it let it sit in your mouth for a second to enjoy the various textures and flavours. How does it feel as it passes over your tongue and goes into your stomach?

You don't need to do this for every bite or even for every meal, but now and then, take a moment to enjoy the experience of eating mindfully, and over time it will become a natural habit. Food provides so much fuel, nourishment, joy and love.

You can practise mindfulness when you are brushing your teeth, going on a car journey, reading a book, typing on the computer, talking to someone, etc. The list is endless.

A great way to start mindfulness practice is to try and stop what you are doing every hour for one minute and be mindful for that minute in your activity. If you have been working on the laptop for an hour, stop for a second and take a breath, and as you begin to type, let go of any distracting thoughts. Look at the keyboard and screen, noticing all the various letters, numbers and symbols, the colours, the text. Look around you. What else do you see? Feel your fingers as you type, notice your chair, your clothes, your mug or bottle, your pens, etc. What can you hear, taste and smell? People talking, your fingers typing, your breathing, the aromas of coffee or plants, etc.

If you've been driving on autopilot, look at the view in front of you. What do you see and notice? What do you feel as you drive? What can you hear?

I can almost hear you say 'I haven't got time to be mindful', but my question would be why are you rushing life? If you are rushing every task, every conversation, every activity, is it because your purpose is to simply get through life? Are you enjoying this process of being constantly busy? You can still do everything you are doing, but by being mindful as much as you can, you will enjoy the beauty of everything that is in front of you and more. That person who smiled as you noticed them on a walk, the colourful flowers emerging through garden walls in the harshest of conditions, that path that was right on your doorstep all this time, the sound of children's conversations, the talk that made a difference to your colleague, the taste of the last biscuit in the tin.

The power of sleep

As we give our time and energy to many things physically and emotionally, we forget that this effort comes from somewhere and that it isn't an endless resource. We often underestimate how important sleep is in giving our body and mind a rest and allowing them to replenish our energy and make repairs where required. Many biological processes, such as cell repair, the release of hormones, energy restoration, protein synthesis, the release of toxic waste and nerve cell communication, occur during the time we are sleeping.

Sometimes we try and get away with as little sleep as we can, watching that extra Netflix movie, finishing off some work, scrolling on our phones, and before we know it, we're hitting our bed and getting off to sleep very late before an early start gets us up again. We wake up tired and go straight into stress and overload mode at the start of the day ahead of us. We overlook the fact that sleep should be seen as being just as important as eating and hydrating.

Research has shown that sleep can impact your immune system, weight, cardiac health, productivity and mood. Sleeping is vital to our survival, and therefore, the amount and the quality of our sleep really do matter.

Let's focus on how the brain is impacted by sleep and how it can impact our emotional well-being. The relationship between sleep and well-being is a close one: lack of sleep, or sleep of poor quality, can impact our mental health, and having poor mental health can make it harder to sleep.

When we are asleep, certain parts of the brain called the amygdala and the hippocampus increase their activity during the different cycles of sleep. By being more active and regulated during sleep, the amygdala can respond in a much calmer way when faced with stress, instead of overreacting, which it does when deprived of sleep. During sleep, the brain is able to process emotional information, and the quality of this processing is again dependent on the amount of sleep we have.

The amygdala is responsible for our emotional responses and uses the time spent sleeping to process our emotions. Have you ever noticed that you are more irritable or easily frustrated and angered when you are sleep-deprived? That's because lack of sleep and poor-quality sleep cause the amygdala to overwork, which in turn causes our emotional responses to intensify.

The prefrontal cortex is also impacted. In contrast to the amygdala, which shapes our emotional responses, it enables us to use logic and reason. The prefrontal cortex and the amygdala work together, but they can't do this productively if we are short of sleep.

Research shows that the period between 10 p.m. and 2 a.m. is the time when the brain can achieve good-quality sleep and focus on healing itself. How you go to sleep really matters. If you have just eaten a heavy meal prior to sleeping, then your brain will spend the first few crucial hours on digesting food instead of healing. If you have watched the world news before retiring, your brain will spend time processing the potentially disturbing images you have seen. If you have been dealing with work issues late into the evening, your brain will still be in a state of stress trying to figure things out.

We can only try to do all we can to ensure we have a good quality and quantity of sleep and give our attention to the following points.

1. Environment

Ensure your room is as zen as it can be for your night-time rest. Use dimmed lights and reduce or eliminate your gadget use, especially in the thirty minutes prior to sleeping. Make sure your pillows, mattress and duvet offer good support and comfort. Some people find that weighted blankets provide extra comfort when sleeping. Block out extra light or extraneous noise as effectively as possible.

2. Nutrition

Limit alcohol and caffeine before bed, and have calming warm drinks like camomile tea instead. Avoid late meals, as these can sometimes cause digestive issues and in turn impact comfort for sleeping.

3. Unwind
Do something to destress and unwind before you sleep so that you are not going to sleep under any emotional stress: take a bath or shower, read, listen to calming music, meditate or write in a journal. Calming essential oils and aromas can play a role here.

4. Routine
Try and keep to the same routine so that your body clock gets used to going to sleep at a certain time and you also look forward to your evening ritual.

5. Exercise
Exercise can also really help us get a good sleep, but try to avoid it very late at night.

6. Avoid stress
Avoid any media distractions prior to bedtime, such as watching the news, scrolling on social media or checking work emails and messages.

It's important to have strong morning and evening routines; I call these the 'bookends' of the day. When you wake up, especially if you're cutting it fine to get yourself ready and you've hit the snooze button multiple times, you are very likely to be in stress mode. You will feel overwhelmed by the day ahead and the rush to get ready as you try to remember everything you need to do, and then you will go straight into the day with your body in a stress-alert cycle. You may feel tired; therefore, you will be irritable, and the smallest triggers will set you off: you may react negatively to situations such as traffic jams or email problems, and this will worsen your already low mood. You may not be able to think as clearly or feel as motivated as you'd like, and conversations with those around you may not be productive. In short, the way you start your day can really impact the rest of it.

If you were to wake up a little earlier than usual (I can hear some of the groans, but hear me out) and have some things in place to allow your mind to feel calm and uplifted, this would have a positive impact on the rest of your day.

Now, trust me when I tell you I was definitely not a morning person and that I very much lived for my sleep – those extra minutes of sleep in the morning were golden. So, what made me give it a go? I was curious about what would happen if I tried. What magical difference, if any, was rising a little earlier going to make to my day? Why couldn't I just find some other time to do the morning things? I had read about the benefits, but I wasn't convinced; however, being on a journey of transformation, I was open to trying it all. I began by waking up at 6 a.m. (the struggle was real), having some water and then going downstairs and doing a guided meditation using an app. I did the meditation for ten minutes. I then made a coffee and sat in silence simply observing my thoughts. At 6.30 a.m., I did a little physical activity – a short core exercise, a HIIT workout or some yoga – for about fifteen minutes.

Those three things – water, meditation and exercise – constituted my routine in the very beginning. At 6.45 a.m., I felt so calm and yet so alive. I got ready peacefully and got the kids ready; the morning didn't feel chaotic with everyone running into each other in every direction. By 9 a.m., I was ready to start my working day, and I felt at ease, I felt peaceful, I felt strong, and I felt good. I was looking forward to the day.

When I started this, I was struggling with anxiety, so for me to approach my day like this was a huge deal. I found I wanted more of the benefits I was beginning to feel, and so I carried on with this practice. My routine has changed over the years. The water and meditation are an absolute must for me. The exercise element changes depending on whether I am going to a class or planning a different workout later in the day; sometimes I read a little instead, sometimes I just observe my thoughts, occasionally I write things down, and sometimes my meditation is a little longer than normal.

Having this morning routine made a huge difference to me, my day, and the quality of my interactions with people around me. It definitely wasn't easy to begin with, but it became easier over time, and the benefit overtook the few painful moments of easing my way out of bed. In fact, I actually began to look forward to it.

In the winter, I may wake up fifteen minutes later, and in the summer, I may wake up earlier. I don't judge myself; I do what I can and aim to continue making small improvements and changes.

So, if you can wake up even ten or fifteen minutes

earlier than usual and implement one or two things to start your day positively, that will have a huge impact.

There will be many reasons why you may think this is not for you. You may be having broken sleep because of the need to look after your children or because you work late into the night. Perhaps you work different shifts or have other issues. In this case, you could limit the new routine to once or twice a week, or wake up just three minutes earlier than usual and sit on your bed and take ten deep breaths and say an affirmation ten times. Small steps are fine. You don't have to go from 0 to 100 mph overnight; find a manageable way to make progress step by step.

Suggestions for your morning routine

(Here, you can pick what works for you or what you think you may enjoy. The key is to try things out for a consistent length of time to notice the impact they are having.)

Wake up earlier by a certain number of minutes.

Hydrate with warm water – have some nearby in a thermos flask.

Practise some deep breathing for one minute.

Choose an affirmation and repeat it ten times.

Do a mini meditation.

Exercise – whether it's running up and down the stairs, following a YouTube workout, going out for a walk, or making a visit to the gym.

Do some yoga.

Set some intentions for the day.

Nourish your body with food.

Practise gratitude.

Take a cold shower.

What will you do in your morning routine? Write down your plan.

I will begin my morning routine on (date):

I will set my alarm to wake up at (time):

The three things I will try to do in my morning routine (feel free to add more) are:

1.

2.

3.

I am going to try these because:

Suggestions for your bedtime routine

Our bedtime routine is just as important as our morning routine because we need our mind and body to wind down ready to enjoy good-quality sleep. If our day has been busy, stressful or exciting, our mind will constantly be replaying the day's actions and conversations: what went well and what could have gone better. And when we are done analysing all that, we go straight into thinking about the next day's tasks.

The evening is when we need to be relaxed, destressed and calm in order to get a good sleep that will enable us to take on another day positively and productively.

You could end your evening by:

- Having a warm bath or a hot shower;
- Practising gratitude;
- Having a warm drink;
- Reading a book;
- Listening to a podcast;
- Journaling;
- Avoiding scrolling on social media;
- Ensuring you are in bed at a time that will allow you to get enough hours of sleep.

The three things I will add to my evening routine:

1.

2.

3.

I will aim to be in bed by (time):

I will begin this on (date):

The reason I am ensuring I have a good evening routine is:

The power of nutrition

The type of food we eat and the liquids we drink can impact how we function mentally and physically. How we nourish ourselves affects whether we feel energetic, fit and alert or lethargic, tired and in a low mood.

Good nutrition supports our physical health, from reducing the risk of certain conditions such as diabetes, stroke, osteoporosis, heart disease, high blood pressure and high cholesterol to enabling us to be physically active and able to undertake a wide range of activities.

Good nutrition can also positively impact our mental health. When we don't eat properly or enough, or we don't stay hydrated, this can lead to low mood, tiredness, irritation and frustration. So, whether you are a foodie or simply eat to fill a hole, it is important to notice what, and when and how, you eat, and to reflect on why you are eating in order to avoid eating purely from habit or from boredom.

Become more mindful about your eating. Are you a

comfort eater? Do you eat when you are feeling low or tired? When you are celebrating, do you see food as a reward? These habits can lead to unhappiness, as you often feel guilty for eating snacks or hit a low after you have had a sugar spike. Eat snacks that you enjoy in moderation. Additionally, try to substitute food treats for something different: a long bath, a movie night, a date with a friend, candles and music. Remember also that it's important not to pass on undesirable habits to any little people in our life by always rewarding our children's good behaviour, achievements and milestones with edible treats.

If we are consistently making poor choices, eating on the go, grabbing snacks and eating processed convenience foods and takeaways daily, this will have a negative impact on our health. If we are consciously making an effort to eat healthy, nutrient-dense foods and having a good dietary balance, then we will feel good as we do so, and that will be reflected in our daily physical activities.

Certain foods can lift our mood: proteins, fermented foods, nuts, good fats, oats and other whole grains, berries, beans and lentils, and – my favourite – dark chocolate. There are many more, so do take a moment to research the foods that promote a good mood.

We are living busy lives, and sometimes, searching out healthy foods and looking at what we are eating can be low on our list of priorities. It is also very tempting to order fast food nowadays, as we have access to a huge number of instant-access food delivery apps and drive-throughs. Life can be crazy and chaotic, and it is absolutely okay to get those takeaways and convenience meals occasionally, but ensure you are planning and preparing good food choices for the majority of your week.

The power and control lie in us. Food also has vibrational energy: fried or processed foods will have low energy in their production and manufacture. Plant-based foods that have been produced by people who have lovingly looked after their crops and plants will have high vibrations. The energy from your food is ingested by you and carried within you.

Toxins can be present in your system. How much water are you giving your body to flush out these toxins on a daily basis? Are you drying the body out with caffeinated drinks or hydrating it with water?

It is really important to assess what you are putting into your body each day and across the week. You can choose to eat anything, but are you keeping a good balance? Are you getting enough vitamins, minerals and nourishment from all food groups?

You don't have to be a chef or an expert cook, and cooking doesn't have to be time consuming. Simple stir-fry meals, blended soups, boiled pasta with vegetables, bean wraps, protein with steamed vegetables: all of these can be prepared in fifteen to twenty minutes. There are many fifteen-minute recipes available in cookbooks and online, and many people find it very convenient to use commercially available food boxes that provide precisely assembled ingredients and recipes to kick start their cooking experience.

If you are feeling tired or stressed or overwhelmed, don't immediately blame your work, your daily chores, your family, etc. The culprit could well be the quality of your nutrition.

Remember that you are what you eat – and also what you think. Your nutrition and your physical exercise regime affect your mental well-being, and your mental well-being affects your physical condition. It's vital to look after both.

Well-being exercise

Write down what you ate yesterday:

Breakfast:
-
-

Lunch:
-
-

Dinner:
-
-

Snacks:
-
-

Write down what fluids you had yesterday:
-
-
-

Try and look back at the last week and do the same for each day.

On a scale of 1 to 10 (10 being fantastic), how well balanced do you think your meals are?

Could you make any small changes for the future? Perhaps you could eat less or more of something. Consider swapping items. For example, you might swap that third biscuit for a cracker or some fruit, or swap a third normal cup of tea for herbal tea. Perhaps you could increase your one glass of water to two. Could you order fewer takeaways?

Try to write down these amendments and incorporate them in a new weekly meal plan.

Notice the changes in your mood and energy levels as you enjoy the benefits of these adjustments. Write them down in a journal to record the changes you experience over time.

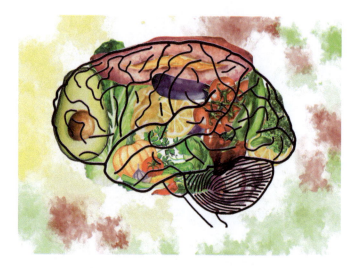

The power of exercise

Exercise: is it something you know you need to do more of but keep putting off? Or do you do the bare minimum? Or are you someone who loves it and has set workouts and a regimented fitness routine that works for you?

If you happen to be someone who doesn't really like exercising, I think it's important to know about the incredible impact exercise has, not just on physical health but on your mental health too.

Exercise can help reduce stress and improve your sleep, your mood, your memory and your overall positivity. When you are stressed, you may experience poor sleep and a lack of appetite; however, exercising releases hormones called endorphins, which act as a natural painkiller and support the body in reducing its stress. Exercise reduces anxiety by making your brain focus on a different activity, allowing the mind to reduce its overload and giving it time to process and respond to any situation.

Any form of physical activity can initiate the release of feel-good hormones from the brain, whether you are walking up and down the stairs, going for a walk around the block, participating in an exercise class or working out at the gym. You may have noticed that when you have been for a walk or done some exercise, your mood has changed from what it previously was as endorphins and serotonin have been released. You will also feel like you have accomplished something, and so another hormone, dopamine, is released, once again making you feel good. Doing exercise first thing in the morning can really set you up for a productive, feel-good day where you will become more motivated and energised to do other tasks.

If exercise isn't your thing, start with small, manageable steps. Find a support partner to help you track your activities, and do something you enjoy. Enjoying what you do is vital. Go for weekly walks with friends or family. Use programmes like Couch to 5k to get you started. Join a class that feels like fun for you, whether that's yoga, Zumba, running, HIIT or something else. There's so much to choose from and so much you can try online too if going to an activity in person feels a little daunting to begin with.

Climb the stairs a few times, and increase this each week. Alternatively, do arm exercises with some tin cans. Consider recruiting a personal trainer to support you if you want something more bespoke. It's known that when you participate in group activities, team sports and fitness communities, you feel a sense of belonging, you feel supported and encouraged, and you have the opportunity to develop new friendships.

There is always something you can do at any level of ability, and there is always something that you will enjoy. There is nothing stopping you apart from you, and remember that it simply starts with ONE. One press-up, one sit-up, one step, one cycle ride, one run, one walk, one weights session: just one will get you started on the journey.

Regular exercise can boost self-confidence and self-esteem as you achieve fitness goals, improve your physical abilities and experience the positive effects of physical activity on your body and mind.

When exercise isn't something you enjoy, it's common to find every excuse not to do it, the most common one being a lack of time and the consequent prioritising of other activities before a workout is even considered. Another barrier may be that you feel too 'tired' to exercise, but exercise can really energise you and get you back on track in feeling more alert and awake. I have begun to do ten thousand steps a day, and it most definitely wasn't something I was motivated to do initially, but I knew it would make a big difference to my health. Ever since I began doing it, I have felt amazing. I go out rain or shine, and the combination of being in nature and physical movement really elevates my mood too.

Your future self and body will thank you for it when you are still mobile and able because you kept yourself in good physical health. It will make a world of difference.

Even if you are faced with illnesses, you will have a much higher chance of fighting them because you looked after your physical health all this time.

The power of visualisation

As people often say, you have to see it to believe it, and in the case of visualisation, you have to see it in your own mind. Your brain works towards the images and words you give it and will do everything it can to support the information you are feeding it; therefore, it is important to have clear images of what it is that you would like to feel, to be and to achieve. People who are anxious or worried may visualise their problems, fear and difficulties; the brain then uses this information to amplify those images through negative emotions and actions. They consequently feel withdrawn and unable to take the necessary steps to be able to move forward positively. Positive-minded people will visualise happier images, and this leads to them feel more motivated and inspired to continue moving forward positively and optimistically.

The power of visualisation is incredible because our imagination is limitless. We can imagine absolutely anything, and that being the case, you can start creating the person you want to be and the life you want to have. Our conscious mind is forever putting limits on our abilities: 'I can't do this because I don't have the time.' 'I don't have enough money or the right skills.' Our imagination can let all of that go, and we can dream of limitless possibilities. And these dreams have a chance of becoming reality when accompanied by positive thought, motivation, determination and discipline.

Did you know that, as an aspiring artist, Jim Carrey wrote himself a cheque for $10 million? He kept it in his wallet whilst visualising becoming a famous actor. He was paid exactly that amount some years later for the movie *Dumb and Dumber*. This is not to say that everyone who does the same will receive a huge amount of money, but by visualising something and believing it can happen, we can increase the chance of it manifesting. Always focus on what you *do* want and not what you *don't* want.

A tennis player going into a match visualises on-court scenarios and trains their mind to believe that they are feeling strong, that they will see every ball coming at them, that their reflexes and reactions will be at a peak, that their energy is flowing, that they know their opponent's every move and that they are ready for this game. They visualise themselves playing against their opponent in the way I have just described. They gift themselves powerful images not only of holding the winner's trophy but also of the journey towards it.

Whether they win or not, they will have gone into that match giving it everything. If they went in thinking they were not on form or they weren't good enough, they would see themselves missing shots and making errors, and their energy would not be there in the match; they would doubt themselves. Their focus and clarity would be hazy and their chances of victory diminished.

If I am about to give a talk, I visualise my audience. I visualise myself walking around and talking, engaging with the crowd, making them feel valid, letting them know I see them and that I am grateful they are there. I visualise myself smiling and laughing, easing any nerves and tension. I see myself speaking clearly and concisely remembering the information I want to deliver. I even visualise the feeling of being content at the end knowing I gave my very best.

Visualising who you want to be, what you want to feel, the clothes you intend to wear and the environment you want to see yourself in will start moving your present self towards those goals.

The benefits of visualisation include the ability to give ourselves a greater chance to achieve our goals by mentally rehearsing the processes and pathways involved. It offers us clearer intentions, focus and motivation. Many athletes and professional sports people use visualisation to raise their performance levels. By rehearsing movements, strategies and outcomes they can improve muscle memory and confidence, and visualising positive outcomes and possibilities enables them to enhance their performance. We too can derive similar benefits from visualisation.

Let's practise some visualisation. Find a comfortable spot to sit. Take some deep breaths. Think about what it is you would like to see, feel and achieve. This doesn't always have to be a specific goal; it could be about changing an aspect of your character or the way you approach situations. You might, for example, become angry quickly and want to be able to control your temper, or you might have a tendency to procrastinate and wish to feel more motivated and productive.

Close your eyes and see yourself taking the steps towards being who you want to be. What are you wearing? Where are you? Who's around you, if anyone? Let us say you are working on managing your temper. You come across a frustrating situation. Visualise yourself taking some deep breaths and taking a step back, processing the situation quietly and then making a calm, unstressed response. Visualise yourself being productive in that situation, and smiling at yourself afterwards, feeling calm and serene.

Let's now imagine instead that you're working on procrastination. Visualise yourself feeling energised at the start of the day, wearing clothes that lift your mood. You're writing down a to-do list. Imagine yourself working through the to-do list, ticking items off as you go along. Visualise yourself feeling good and motivated to keep going; you have a cup of tea to reward your morning's hard work and carry on again after ten minutes. You visualise yourself looking at the clock, and it's 4 p.m. You've accomplished so much; you feel great, you feel lighter, and you've confirmed to yourself that you can do it.

Maybe you want to work on becoming fitter and healthier. Visualise yourself eating nourishing, colourful, vibrant foods. If you happen to have a sweet tooth, see those sugary foods shrinking in size or with mould or fungus growing on them. Make the image appear unattractive. Now make the image of the healthy foods bold, large, shiny, fresh and appetising. See yourself opening the fridge and choosing fresh, healthy options. See yourself in the mirror wearing your perfect outfit and feeling strong and beautiful.

Take a moment to visualise a scenario for yourself now.

Hormone hacks

Hormones are chemical messengers created in the endocrine system that travel in the bloodstream and support various bodily processes. There are certain hormones that can support mood and well-being; these 'happy' hormones can be remembered by the acronym DOSE, standing for dopamine, oxytocin, serotonin and endorphins.

Dopamine: the reward hormone

Dopamine is known as the reward hormone. It is associated with pleasure and motivation and is released when you achieve or accomplish something. When released, it makes you feel good, and you are motivated to continue with the actions that caused this sensation. If you are procrastinating and lack motivation or you require support with focus and concentration, then you need to stimulate dopamine production.

Ways to stimulate the production of dopamine:
1. Celebrate the little wins in life;
2. Make a to-do list and tick off items from it through the day;
3. Break down large goals into bite-size chunks so you can tick those off as you achieve them;
4. Engage in self-care and journaling;
5. Involve yourself in rewarding activities that you enjoy, such as hobbies and sports;
6. Listen to music.

Oxytocin: the bonding hormone

This hormone is essential when you are building relationships, connecting and bonding, and it is essential during childbirth. It can help bring people closer together.

Ways to stimulate the production of oxytocin:
1. Snuggle with a pet animal;
2. Send text messages to check in on people;
3. Give praise and compliments;
4. Hold hands and be affectionate with your partner;
5. Give hugs;
6. Cook and share food together with your family;
7. Engage in meaningful and purposeful conversations with others;
8. Engage in activities that allow people to bond, such as team-building exercises or games.

Serotonin: the mood regulator

This hormone helps you elevate your mood, as well as supporting digestion, sleep, memory and focus. If you want to reduce your anxiety or your low mood, regulate positive emotions and increase your overall well-being and happiness, then you need to stimulate serotonin production.

Ways to stimulate the production of serotonin:
1. Take some vitamin D;
2. Do exercise – ideally an aerobic activity;
3. Be in nature – go for a walk;
4. Practise journaling;
5. Practise mindfulness and meditation;
6. Read motivational books or listen to podcasts;
7. Engage in self-care practices.

Endorphins: the natural pain relievers

Endorphins act as natural pain relievers when your body is experiencing physical pain or chronic stress.

Ways to stimulate the production of endorphins:
1. Do some exercise;
2. Laugh – watch a comedy with friends;
3. Be creative;
4. Try acupuncture;
5. Have a massage;
6. Burn essential oils, especially lavender oil;

7. Have a warm bath;
8. Eat spicy food.

To summarise: These hormones are complex, and they interact with each other and with other neurotransmitters in the brain. The release and regulation of these hormones are influenced by various factors, including genetics, lifestyle, environment and individual differences. Engaging in activities that promote the release of these neurotransmitters, such as exercise, social interactions and enjoyable experiences, can contribute to positive emotions and a sense of well-being.

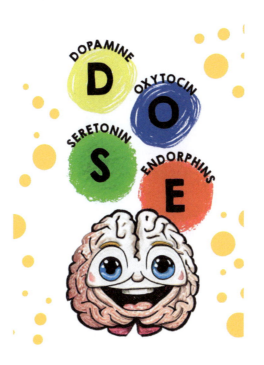

The power of journaling

Journaling is a very powerful way to release our thoughts freely and without judgement. There is no one watching us or reading what we write, and therefore, this should give us a great sense of liberation as we place our feelings on paper instead of keeping our emotions pent up in our minds and hearts.

Some people love journaling. Others have doubts or are unsure about it. And some just don't really know where to begin. I was in all of these categories at various points in my life until something powerful changed for me, which I will explain later on.

The value of journaling is that it facilitates not just a release of emotions and ideas, but also a different way of looking at our thoughts. When we are constantly thinking about things, we can create a mountain of obstacles in our mind that lead to stress, overload, fear and anxiety. If we aren't comfortable speaking to someone about our emotions, then writing them down offers a different way to process them. Often when we write things down, it gives us a better chance to process, reflect on, assess and understand different areas of our life.

Using a diary, a notebook or a phone calendar, many people will write down shopping lists, jobs for the day, things they need to pack, reminders, etc. This helps us to prioritise things and to manage and navigate tasks; it also gives us reminders of what to do and when. Best of all, you can tick those items off once they're complete. Imagine having all those lists and tasks just in your head – it would be impossible for anything to run smoothly.

Writing about your worries, moods and emotions can be therapeutic. You can validate your feelings, you can begin to understand them, you can think about how you would rather feel, and you can consider ways to move forward. Writing down your joy, achievements and feel-good moments is also important because it validates every aspect of your life and illustrates how far you have come in all areas.

Now initially, I was never one for journaling. I didn't see the point, because I used to talk so much about my feelings and my life (my poor husband had his ear chewed off daily), and so journaling didn't feel necessary to me. However, there was a point when I thought I would give it a go: there was no harm in trying, and maybe it would do some good. At all events, unless I tried, I would never know. It really is important to be open to ideas as you never know the difference they might make.

So, I got a notebook and thought I would start by writing out any struggles I was going through, then

I wrote about what I would like to achieve, and then I wrote about things I was grateful for. I didn't think too much; there was no neat ordering of the information. I just wrote whatever was entering my head and heart and let it flow onto the paper. No one was going to read it, and therefore, like the saying 'dance like no one is watching', I journaled like no one was watching.

It felt good to do, and then I put it away and didn't really think about it. In due course, I decided to journal again. I found a new notebook (possibly because I couldn't find that first one) and wrote in it again in the same way. I didn't feel particularly lighter or moved in any way, but I kept the practice going regularly. Almost a year later, something amazing happened. I happened to find my original journal and I opened it to read it, and wow, some of the things I had written were so raw. I looked at some of the things that had been upsetting me, things I hadn't achieved but wanted to, and the other thoughts I must have had at the time.

Now one year on from that journal entry, I had actually achieved 75 per cent of the goals written there, and things that I had thought were not available or achievable had actually been accomplished. We often glide through life widening our goalposts, wanting more, thinking that what we do have isn't enough or that we could have done better, unaware of the truth that just a year ago, we would have dreamt of being in the position we're in today. It also made me realise just how far I had come with my mindset and how what once used to upset or impact me no longer did.

It was so wonderful to read, and it really made me think that we should never forget how far we have come and how much we have accomplished, how five years ago we would have dreamt of having some of the things we have today. We often don't realise our progress, because we continue moving forward on to the next thing. We may recall some of the big moments and milestones in our life, but journaling really allows you to see in detail just how far you have come, reminding you of the small changes and adjustments you've made, and the grit and grace you've shown as you worked through difficult situations in the journey you have been on.

So, I would highly recommend journaling. I wish I had started it earlier. Write about everything and anything, what you are feeling today, what you are dealing with, your emotions, your highs and lows and everything in between. You don't have to write in your journal daily; it's your choice. Some write daily, some write weekly, some pick it up as and when they feel drawn to it. It may feel unfamiliar at first, but you will soon find your flow, and it will become a familiar part of your journey. You will be amazed at what you read back to yourself six months down the line.

Well-being exercise

Purchase a journal or a notebook. You can purchase journals that have prompts on each page making it easier to fill them in. Some people prefer this format, while others like to write freestyle, so experiment, and see what your preference is.

Find a time when you have fifteen or twenty minutes and when everything is calm and you are distraction-free. Some like to do this first thing in the morning, some in the evening before bedtime. Find what works for you.

You may want to create an atmosphere by lighting a candle or an incense stick to add aromas.

Then, let the words flow, and write whatever comes to your mind. Some of your reflections may include:

- Your day so far;
- Your mood and emotions;
- What's been going well for you;
- What's causing you any stress, worry or anxiety;
- Any people who may be causing you hurt;
- What you would like to feel more or less of;
- What you would like to achieve;
- The people and things you are grateful for.

Journaling can provide many benefits. It can reduce your stress and anxiety; improve your clarity, focus and memory; and facilitate your self-reflection and your personal growth.

Embrace your perfectly imperfect self: revisited

Now that you have read these chapters, and perhaps learnt some things about yourself and pondered further questions in the process, I want you to remember to treat yourself with kindness and to really cut yourself some slack; give yourself a break in this game of life. You are aiming for progress, not perfection, so on the journey, embrace your perfectly imperfect self.

The expression 'perfectly imperfect' refers to the idea that imperfections and flaws are an inherent and an acceptable part of being human. They do not diminish one's worth or value. We need to accept and appreciate imperfection as a natural and beautiful aspect of life.

Here are some definitions of what 'perfectly imperfect' signifies.

Embracing flaws: It acknowledges that nobody and nothing is flawless or without imperfections. It recognises that imperfections are what make individuals unique and authentic. Instead of inviting us to strive for an unattainable and idealised notion of perfection, it promotes self-acceptance and self-love despite imperfections. Being authentic is living purposefully and truthfully.

Recognising beauty in imperfection: 'Perfectly imperfect' highlights the notion that imperfections can be beautiful and valuable. It suggests that imperfections can add character, depth and charm to a person, a situation or an object. It encourages us to see the beauty in the uniqueness and individuality that imperfections bring.

Acceptance of oneself and others: It promotes accepting people, including oneself, as they are, with all their flaws and shortcomings. It encourages a compassionate and non-judgemental attitude towards oneself and others, recognising that everyone has their own struggles, limitations and imperfections. Often, we fall in love with people who are themselves, who have their own quirky ways or endearing mannerisms that are unique to them. They are not trying to be anyone but themselves.

Embracing growth and learning: 'Perfectly imperfect' acknowledges that imperfections provide opportunities for growth, self-improvement and learning. It suggests that mistakes, failures and setbacks are valuable experiences that can lead to personal development and resilience. It encourages embracing challenges and using them as stepping stones to progress.

Embracing vulnerability: Recognising and accepting imperfections often requires the admission of vulnerability. Embracing our imperfections means being willing to show our true selves, including our weaknesses and insecurities. It involves being open and authentic, allowing others to see and accept us as we are.

Letting go of perfectionism: Perfectionism is the tendency to strive for flawlessness and to set unrealistically high standards for oneself. The concept of 'perfectly imperfect' challenges the notion of perfectionism and encourages letting go of the need to be perfect. It promotes a healthier and more balanced approach to self-improvement and self-acceptance.

Resisting societal pressures: Society often promotes ideals of perfection, whether in terms of appearance, achievements or lifestyles. Embracing the idea of being 'perfectly imperfect' means resisting these societal pressures and defining our own standards of worth and success. It involves valuing authenticity, self-compassion and genuine connections over external expectations.

Fostering resilience and self-compassion: Accepting imperfections allows us to cultivate resilience and self-compassion. When we acknowledge and embrace our imperfections, we become better equipped to handle setbacks, failures and criticism. We can respond to challenges with kindness and understanding, treating ourselves with the same compassion we would offer to others.

Celebrating growth and progress: The concept of 'perfectly imperfect' recognises that growth and progress are ongoing journeys. It encourages celebrating the progress we make, even if it's not perfect or linear. By focusing on the process and acknowledging the steps we take, we can appreciate our efforts and the lessons learnt along the way.

Cultivating empathy and acceptance: Embracing our own imperfections can lead to increased empathy with, and acceptance of, others. When we recognise our own flaws and vulnerabilities, we become more understanding and compassionate towards the imperfections of other people. It helps foster a sense of connection and empathy in our relationships and interactions with others.

To summarise, 'perfectly imperfect' reminds us that striving for an unattainable and flawless ideal can be exhausting and unfulfilling. It encourages us to accept ourselves and others with compassion and embrace the growth that comes from our imperfections. It celebrates the uniqueness and authenticity that arise from being human and imperfect. Ultimately, the concept of 'perfectly imperfect' invites us to embrace our human condition with all its strengths, weaknesses and imperfections. It encourages a more authentic way of living, allowing us to appreciate the beauty in imperfection and find value in the journey of self-discovery and growth.

Own your perfectly imperfect self, and embrace your perfectly imperfect life and the perfectly imperfect people in it.

Now what?

You've read the book. Now what? Now it's up to *YOU*.

Reread the chapters addressing areas you need to focus on more; look through the exercises again; and begin to implement the changes you have learnt about.

Now that you have read this book and absorbed the information in it, you have to act on that information. No one can do this but you. If you really want to start experiencing inner happiness, then recognise that the process begins with *YOU*.

Look at exactly where you are right now. What is it that you are feeling and experiencing? Look at your situation and the people around you. How does what you see make you feel?

This is a really nice place to assess your current position using a wheel of life.

Take a look at the wheel below. Consider each section of your life, and give it a score from 1 to 10, with 1 meaning that you are nowhere near where you'd like to be in that area and 10 meaning that it is absolutely perfect.

Now pick three areas that you would like to work on. In each area, write down three action points that will help you start moving your scores to a higher point on your scale. For example, if your relationships scored 4/10, write down three things you could start doing to move that number so it becomes a 6/10 or a 7/10. Do you need to have a conversation with someone? Do you need to reduce contact with someone and delete their number from your phone? Do you need to focus more of your energy on people who are supporting you and less on those who aren't?

Create three action points, being very specific and using some of the 'W' questions below:

- WHY have you chosen that goal to work on?
- WHAT is it that you need to do?
- WHEN can you do this? (Be very specific by adding dates and times.)
- WHO, if anyone, do you need to reach out to for support or have a conversation with?

You can also ask yourself HOW you will know whether you have completed the action points. What would the ideal outcome be? And how would you expect to feel once your objectives were accomplished?

EXAMPLE

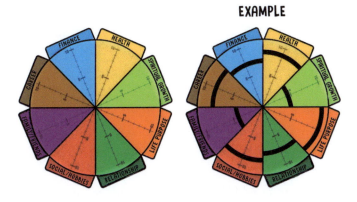

Start implementing small changes in your life: devise a meal plan, ensure you sleep at a reasonable time, write down affirmations and display them on your wall so that you can see them daily, pick up a new hobby and meet like-minded people. These are just a few examples from the limitless range of positive changes that you can start to make now.

It won't be an overnight fix; it will take time, but over this time, you will see some phenomenal transformations that will create the most incredible joy within you. You will begin seeing things from a new perspective; things that used to bother you will no longer even cross your mind, and you will attract the most wonderful experiences and people into your life.

Remember that nothing is easy. You need to be willing to put in the daily inner work and have the regular commitment and discipline to really work on all areas of your life. Remember that you are stronger, more courageous and more resilient than you imagine. You are also more adaptable to change than you realise and way more deserving of happiness than you think.

Everything begins with one thought and one step and one person: *YOU*.

I also want to remind you that your story, like your situations past and present, is unique to you. Therefore, the time you need to process things, figure them out and heal will be unique to you. There is no competition, no race, no need for comparison. There never was and never will be. Take the steps that feel right for you.

Be kind and patient towards yourself on this journey; you are doing amazing, life-transforming work, and it will take time and perseverance. However, what you are about to experience will be phenomenal. You will feel incredible, and the abundance of love and happiness you attract and feel within will be astonishing.

This journey as you dive deeper within yourself will become one of the best adventures you ever embark on. It is a true journey, so enjoy the highs, embrace the lows, and continue to put in the work every day. I am so incredibly excited for you and for what is about to unfold.

About the Author

Sheena Tanna-Shah is a rapid transformation therapy practitioner, a mindfulness, meditation and NLP practitioner, a mindset coach and the author of *Perfectly Imperfect Mum*. She is a motivational speaker, and her work has been featured on *BBC News* and on ITV, as well as in *Hello!* magazine and various other publications. Sheena lives with her husband and two daughters, and *The Power of Being Perfectly Imperfect* is her second published book.

www.inspiring-success.com
Sheena@inspiring-success.com
Instagram: sheenasinspiringsuccess